C000029953

Classics

LEEDS

RUGBY LEAGUE CLUB

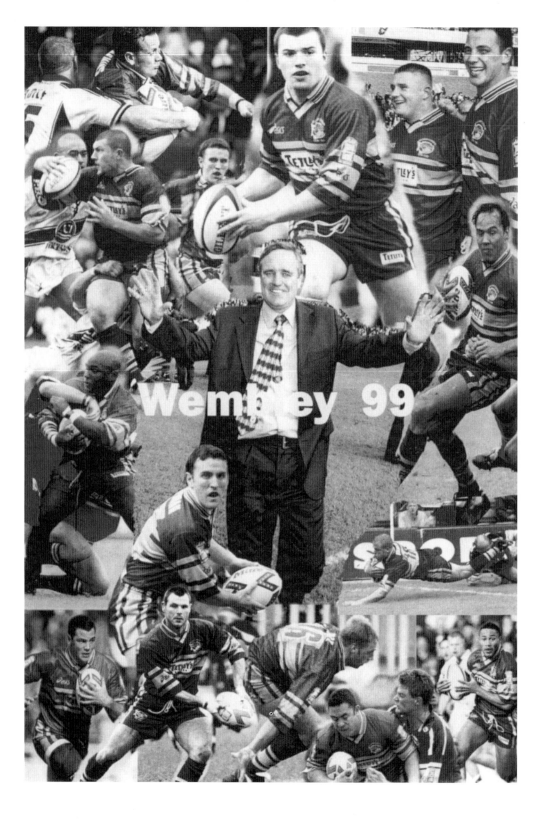

Wembley 99

Classics
LEEDS
RUGBY LEAGUE CLUB

PETER SMITH & PHIL CAPLAN

TEMPUS

For our parents, Brian and Dinah Smith and Geoff and
Gill Caplan, with thanks

In memory of Oscar Caplan, who passed the first ball

First published 2003

Tempus Publishing Limited
The Mill, Brimscombe Port,
Stroud, Gloucestershire, GL5 2QG

© Peter Smith & Phil Caplan, 2003

The right of Peter Smith & Phil Caplan to be identified as the Authors
of this work has been asserted in accordance with the
Copyrights, Designs and Patents Act 1988.

All rights reserved. No part of this book may be reprinted
or reproduced or utilised in any form or by any electronic,
mechanical or other means, now known or hereafter invented,
including photocopying and recording, or in any information
storage or retrieval system, without the permission in writing
from the Publishers.

British Library Cataloguing in Publication Data.
A catalogue record for this book is available from the British Library.

ISBN 0 7524 2740 7

Typesetting and origination by Tempus Publishing Limited
Printed in Great Britain by Midway Colour Print, Wiltshire

Foreword

In the twelve seasons during which I was fortunate enough to don the Leeds colours, I played in a number of matches that could be described as classics. There were the obvious ones, particularly the long-awaited Championship success in 1961 and the victory at Wembley in 1957, but also some lesser encounters, which, for various reasons, hold precious memories.

Some are because of personal scoring exploits, such as the match against Bradford in 1956; others are fondly remembered because we showed tremendous team spirit and will to come up with an unexpected win or a triumph out of adversity. One such game was at the Boulevard in the Challenge Cup earlier that same year. Sportsmen, more than most, know how thin the dividing line is between success and failure, fitness and injury and every time I took the field it was with the intention of leaving an impression.

Playing at Headingley was another joy: the facilities, the atmosphere, the history and the knowledgeable home fans at the famous venue always served to inspire – although that often applied to the opposition as well. I am delighted that books are being written which commemorate the deeds of the past so that future generations can read about the exploits of names they may be familiar with but never saw. The matches that I played in can be found about halfway through this super collection and it is only within the full sweep of history that we can make sense of Leeds' achievements. I hope you enjoy reading about these classic matches as much as I did playing in them.

Lewis Jones,
February 2003

Leeds Rugby League, 1952-1964

Acknowledgements

The various volumes in the late Ken Dalby's excellent *Headingley Story* are an essential source of reference for anyone interested in tracing the history of Leeds Rugby League Club and proved particularly useful in pinpointing key games in the club's early days. The *Yorkshire Evening Post* and *Yorkshire Post* newspapers have covered the club from its inception and have provided an invaluable source of match reports and background information.

We also acknowledge with thanks the use of *Yorkshire Post's* pictures and library facilities. Dave Williams' superb portfolio has supplied many of the modern era photographs in this book. Our thanks go to Stuart Martel for his meticulous proof-reading and to James Howarth, Becky Gadd and everyone at Tempus Publishing for their support, not only for this project but also for the sport of Rugby League. Thanks are also due to Phil Daly, Stuart Duffy, Ray Fletcher, Dave Hadfield, Harry Jepson, Mike Latham, Mick Pope, Simon Reuben and Steve Riding, as well as to Lewis Jones – who provided so many memorable moments in the Leeds Rugby League story – for his foreword.

Classic Matches

1890 *v.* Manningham (Rugby Union)

1895 *v.* Leigh (Northern Union)

1902 *v.* The Rest (Yorkshire Senior Competition)

1907 *v.* New Zealand (Tour match)

1910 *v.* Hull (Challenge Cup final and replay)

1913 *v.* Coventry (Northern Union)

1915 *v.* Wigan (Championship semi-final)

1921 *v.* Dewsbury (Yorkshire Cup final)

1923 *v.* Hull (Challenge Cup final)

1928 *v.* Featherstone Rovers (Yorkshire Cup final)

1931 *v.* Bradford Northern (League)

1932 *v.* Swinton (Challenge Cup final)

1934 *v.* Wakefield Trinity (Yorkshire Cup final, replay and second replay)

1936 *v.* Warrington (Challenge Cup final)

1938 *v.* Hunslet (Championship final)

1938 *v.* Salford (League)

1942 *v.* Halifax (Challenge Cup final)

1947 *v.* Wigan (Challenge Cup quarter-final)

1955 *v.* Hunslet (League)

1956 *v.* Australia (Tour match)

1957 *v.* Halifax (Challenge Cup third round)

1958 *v.* Wakefield Trinity (Yorkshire Cup final)

1961 *v.* Warrington (Championship final)

1964 *v*. Halifax (League)

1968 *v*. Wakefield Trinity (Challenge Cup final)

1969 *v*. Castleford (Championship final)

1969 *v*. Perpignan (European Championship)

1970 *v*. St Helens (Floodlit Trophy final)

1971 *v*. Leigh (Challenge Cup final)

1972 *v*. St Helens (Championship final)

1977 *v*. Widnes (Challenge Cup final)

1978 *v*. St Helens (Challenge Cup final)

1979 *v*. Bradford Northern (Premiership final)

1980 *v*. Blackpool Borough (League Division One)

1981 *v*. Hull KR (Yorkshire Cup final)

1982 *v*. Widnes (Challenge Cup semi-final)

1984 *v*. Widnes (John Player final)

1985 *v*. Bridgend (Challenge Cup preliminary round)

1986 *v*. Hull KR (Challenge Cup semi-final and replay)

1987 *v*. Wigan (John Player semi-final)

1988 *v*. Castleford (Yorkshire Cup final)

1991 *v*. Castleford (Premiership first round)

1994 *v*. St Helens (Challenge Cup semi-final)

1997 *v*. St Helens (Super League)

1997 *v*. Adelaide Rams (World Club Championship)

1998 *v*. Wigan Warriors (Super League)

1998 *v*. Wigan Warriors (Super League Grand Final)

1999 *v*. London Broncos (Challenge Cup final)

2001 *v*. Swinton Lions (Challenge Cup fourth round)

2002 *v*. Bradford Bulls (Challenge Cup fourth round)

Introduction

Leeds has participated in thousands of matches since the club was formed in 1890. This is not an attempt to select the best fifty – that would be an impossible task – instead, it is a collection of games which we feel reflects the highs and lows of every era of the club's remarkable history. It is an entirely subjective choice. We haven't applied any criteria for inclusion in this book, other than the game in question must have been in some way memorable. Most matches don't linger long in the mind. Enjoyable enough while the action is happening, the memory begins to fade as soon as the final whistle is blown. Then there are games that send the crowd home buzzing and which are talked about, reflected on and argued over for years. This is a collection of fifty such games.

Naturally, trophy-winning triumphs figure strongly in this book. The modern generation of Rhinos fans, starved as they have been of success, may find it hard to believe that there was ever a time when it wasn't a question of *if* Leeds would win a trophy in a season, but rather *how many* they would win. Up to 2002, Leeds had won thirty-six finals in different competitions and many of those triumphs are featured here. Of those, the greatest day of all must have been the 1961 Championship victory over Warrington, when the Loiners ended seven decades of waiting to be crowned the top club in Britain. The Challenge Cup final win against London in 1999 will hold a similar place in the hearts of fans born after the glory days of the 1960s and 1970s.

But silverware is not the only ingredient of a classic match. There are also occasions where last-minute drama, a shock result or a heartbreaking defeat make a game an unforgettable occasion. Our initial list of fifty matches was drawn up the day before Leeds Rhinos travelled to Bradford Bulls in the fourth round of the 2002 Challenge Cup competition. We included that tie, when Leeds were rank underdogs, on our list as an act of pre-game bravado and it's fair to say both authors are delighted that it retained its place in the finished volume.

Obviously most of the matches featured in this collection resulted in a Leeds victory, but not all. It is the bad times that make the good ones so enjoyable and it would have been remiss of us not to highlight some spectacularly disappointing results from a Leeds perspective. The final moments of the 1982 Challenge Cup semi-final, when a trip to Wembley was snatched away in the cruellest of circumstances, will be etched forever on the memory of any Leeds fan at the game, watching on television, or, in the case of one of the authors, listening on a radio halfway up a Scottish mountainside. Likewise, the defeat by Blackpool Borough at Headingley in 1980 had to feature, simply as an example of how, when Leeds are involved, nothing can ever be taken for granted.

Other games are memorable simply for the occasion. The Challenge Cup tie against Bridgend in 1985 would have been forgotten, had it not been for a massive pre-match blizzard, which delayed the visiting team's arrival and sparked a huge snowball fight among fans on the Headingley cricket pitch. We have attempted to reflect the roller-coaster story of the Leeds club right from its formation in 1890, and sadly we have had to leave out many matches that would have been worthy of inclusion had there been room for them. This is an entirely personal choice, and no doubt every Leeds fan will have their own opinions of which classic matches should feature. Whether you agree or disagree with our selection, we hope this collection will provoke debate and revive memories and in some way help to preserve the rich history of one of British sport's great clubs.

Victorious on the Town Hall steps in 1977, the homecoming celebrations are led by legendary kit man Harvey Standeven (front row, centre – fist raised).

Leeds v. Manningham

20 September 1890
Headingley

Northern Union
Referee: Baron Kilner (Wakefield)

Controversy reigned as Leeds moved into their new surroundings in Headingley, referred to at the time as 'without doubt one of the best grounds in the county in every respect'. In the week leading up to the historic first match there, letters appeared in the local newspapers complaining about the noise of the carts continually running through the streets taking materials to and from the venue and the amount of debris littering the surrounding area. Despite the ceaseless endeavour to transform the former Lot 17a of the Cardigan Estate, the ground was not completed for this inaugural clash – the banking around the sides remained incomplete and the stand on the Burley End had yet to be constructed. Nevertheless, the pitch and its surrounds looked in superb condition despite heavy downpours in the week prior to the game.

Not surprisingly, the occasion proved to be a tremendous draw with the crowd estimated as one of the best gates ever at a sporting event in the city. That was the cause of the second bone of contention with the club making an unheralded distinction on the morning of the encounter – in the columns of the *Yorkshire Post* and once fans had poured into the enclosure – between guinea and 5s members. The former were given access to the central third of the grandstand with the best view of the action while the latter were expected to fill the ends. They objected and a number of them climbed the slight wooden partitions that marked out the different areas causing mass disturbance before the teams came out. It was only halted by the arrival of the police who cleared the invaders and restored order, although numerous furious arguments continued to erupt throughout the ensuing action. Even the members of the press were caught up in the acrimony when first they were denied access to the stand and then, once they were settled, found that the position of their designated desks meant they were unable to see the play because of the massed ranks in front of them. Arrangements were hastily made to give them a viewing area but the combined commotion caused the kick-off to be delayed by forty minutes.

The other reason for the mass attendance was the form shown by the newly constituted Leeds side in their opening two games of the campaign. A fortnight earlier, Otleyites had been beaten at the home of the former St John's club (with whom Leeds had amalgamated) on Cardigan Fields, Headingley being unavailable owing to an athletics fixture. The following Saturday, reigning champions Park Avenue had been defeated in Bradford in a performance that gained widespread acclaim, and the Valley Paraders from Manningham – who were eventually to turn to soccer as Bradford City – were expected to provide another stern derby test. When the sides were eventually led out, they were greeted with tumultuous cheers, the hosts attired in their new colours of terracotta and green. Both were at full strength, with Leeds including half-back Field from Wortley and Firth coming into the visiting three-quarter line, Carey and Harrison getting a start for them in the forwards.

It fittingly fell to Leeds captain and loose-forward Load to put the first boot to ball to kick off proceedings after Leeds had won the toss and chosen to play with the strong wind and sun at their backs. Pocock initiated the opening attack down the middle before Leeds forward Claude Sumner gained possession but then sent the ball into touch. Diminutive Ike Newton and Robertshaw took the ball to the Leeds line, with first a penalty for off-side and then a fine kick by Field clearing the danger. The visitors were caught off-side, Sumner taking the free-kick but Firth burst clear for Manningham only for Mark Fletcher to make a fine tackle. Sumner seemed to be involved in everything, winning Leeds a line-out, but more concerted pressure by the Paraders saw Fletcher forced to touch down behind his own line and concede a minor.

Leeds 1-1-1   Manningham 0-0-2

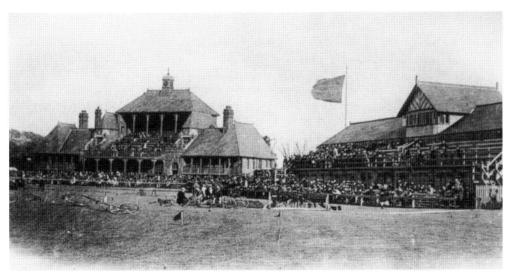

The new showpiece arena opens, playing host to rugby, cricket, athletics and cycling events.

Play was halted for a while when one of the Manningham players required treatment, Leeds prop Hoyle making a fine break, carried on by Fletcher on the resumption. Loiners' second-row George Naylor slipped a great pass to his prop Broadbent and the former Wortley man powered downfield with the crowd frantically cheering his every step before Leeds were credited with a minor. Much of the remainder of the half was spent in midfield, the visiting pack performing well as a unit, Leeds relying on individual bursts from Tommy Summersgill and Southall. Centre Fletcher was having a massive influence and rapidly becoming a supporters' favourite and it was his well-timed break and pass that sent Naylor in at the corner for the first try, Fletcher's fine conversion attempt from the touchline just drifting wide amid tremendous cheering.

The remainder of the half saw the hosts on top with their forwards producing some fine inter-passing and full-back Wilkinson proving an ever-increasing threat. The smart footwork of the Manningham scrummagers saw them open the second period with territorial dominance, but another long-range break by Broadbent, carried on by Naylor and Hoyle, saw Todd denied and Field just fail to re-gather his clever kick. The visitors were saved by two free-kicks, one from a line-out, which took them back into centre field, but they were unable to master the home defence whose counter was dramatic. Todd wriggled free from two tacklers and found Fletcher, who gave Summersgill the time and space to drop a goal. Manningham roused themselves for one final tilt, rushing to the Leeds line and forcing a minor, but the home defence remained resolute with Summersgill, Southall and Wilkinson on Heaton pulling off noteworthy tackles on their own line. Another injury break halted the visitors' momentum and Leeds cleared to halfway with a fine dribble by Naylor. From the scrum, lively Manningham half Pocock fed Newton on the wing and he seemed a certain scorer, only for Southall to prevent the try with a diving tackle that ensured a christening win. Leeds won their next two matches, but the season tailed off thereafter as the early promise associated with their prestigious venue wore off.

Leeds: Wilkinson – back; Southall, Fletcher, Summersgill – three-quarter backs; Burrell, Field – half-backs; Broadbent, Fowler, Hoyle, Hudson, Naylor, Sumner, Todd, Wood, Load – forwards.

Manningham: Brown – back; Newton, Robertshaw, Firth – three-quarter backs; Pocock, Beardsall – half-backs; Holmes, Toothill, Hardaker, Heaton, Boulton, Brayshaw, Clegg, Carey, Graham – forwards.

LEIGH v. LEEDS

7 September 1895   Northern Union
Mather Lane   Referee: Mr Wilcox

Leeds' debut in the Northern Union was a leap into the unknown in more ways than one. The Loiners' first game as a rebel club was away to Leigh on 7 September 1895 and travelling over the Pennines to play rugby was a novel experience. The Leeds team left the city on the 1.40 p.m. train and didn't arrive at their Lancashire destination until 4 p.m. – an hour after the game was due to kick off. After the match they boarded the 7.50 p.m. train out of Leigh, eventually arriving back in Leeds after midnight. It was quite an adventure and Leeds' traumatic journey raised serious questions over whether a cross-Pennine competition could ever flourish. The problems getting to the match caused almost as many headlines as the action on the field and serious concerns were raised about how eastern outpost Hull would fare when they faced games in Lancashire.

Leeds' first-ever game against Leigh was the culmination of years of unrest between northern clubs and the southern-based Rugby Football Union. When the Northern Union split from the RFU in August 1895, Leeds was one of the founder members of the new competition. Throughout the late nineteenth century, there was growing animosity between the Rugby Union bigwigs, based in London, and the working class clubs of northern England. Rugby Union was an entirely amateur sport and the game's administrators, largely drawn from public schools and universities, were determined to keep it that way. Players from clubs in the north were recruited from mills, coal mines and other businesses and had to ask for time off work to play. The suggestion that clubs should be allowed to compensate players for wages lost when playing rugby – broken-time payments – was greeted with outrage by the sport's governors.

The matter came to a head in 1895, when clubs in the north decided to break away, enabling them to make broken-time payments to players. At a historic meeting at the George Hotel, Huddersfield, on 29 August 1895, the Northern Union was formed. The RFU season had been due to begin in mid-September, but NU officials decided to kick off their campaign early. The day before the first round of matches was staged, frantic meetings were held to agree on playing rules, the registration of players and the formation of a referees' panel. Initially, it was agreed that the laws of the game would be unchanged. It was two years before the new sport began to evolve away from Rugby Union, with the abolition of line-outs and changes in scoring.

Leeds and Leigh were each forced to field an under-strength team in their first game as players decided whether they were prepared to take part in the new competition. The fear was that once they lost their 'amateur' status by playing in the rebel league they would become outcasts, with no way back into Rugby Union or any other amateur sport. Among those unable to play were Leeds stalwart Tommy Summersgill, a champion cyclist who was awaiting that sport's governing body's opinion on his new 'professional' status. Leigh were tricky debut opponents, top of the Lancashire First Division and rated as the toughest pack west of the Pennines. The game kicked off at 4.40 p.m. on a warm summer's afternoon and the crowd of 2,500 was one of the lowest of the day, although Leeds were reported to have been greeted by 'hearty cheers' when they eventually stepped off the train.

Leigh officials had been hoping for a gate of 5,000 and were upset that a clash with neighbours Tyldesley's game against Manningham kept the crowd down and deprived both home clubs of valuable income. That was a common occurrence in the early days of the Northern Union, when fixtures were drawn up at short notice. Mark Fletcher and H. Parfitt were to the fore for Leeds, with new recruits C. Hills, from North Durham, and Goodall, from

Leigh 3   Leeds 6

Leeds began their Northern Union existence with away games against Leigh, Widnes and Batley before returning to their new palatial home to take on Brighouse and Hull, winning four of the five matches.

Yorkshire College, impressing with their skilful play. Half-backs J. Bastow and J. Midgley saw more of the ball than their opposite numbers, but the *Yorkshire Evening Post's* reporter at the opening game complained that their old habit of holding on to it longer than was necessary had resurfaced. Behind the halves, F. Wright, H. Hainstock, J. Clarkson and veteran Bob Walton – who had replaced Summersgill in the side – defended strongly and showed some smart touches, although Walton put Leeds under pressure with his tendency to take unnecessary risks. Leeds' historic victory was secured by tries from Bastow, following a forward rush, and Parfitt, who touched down after chasing Walton's kick. The hosts dominated in the forwards but could not turn pressure into points, managing their only score ten minutes from time when Tommy Taylor broke away from a scrum near the Leeds line and rounded Walker to touch down in the corner.

Professionalism remained illegal under NU rules, although broken-time payments were allowed. Ironically, two years after the great split it was revealed that the amount of money spent by Leeds on broken-time payments had actually fallen since the formation of the Northern Union. The Leeds committee's decision to throw their lot in with the new competition wasn't met with total approval. A special general meeting was held at Headingley on 4 October, but the committee won a vote of confidence by 66 votes to 18. The first season saw Leeds record a financial loss of £272 with membership of the club falling from 1,291 to 402, with an average attendance of 3,900, but support for the Northern Union was expressed at the end-of-season annual meeting. On the field, Leeds finished the campaign with a disappointing record of 20 wins, 3 draws and 19 defeats from their 42 games, scoring 258 points and conceding 247. The club's first Northern Union defeat was 11-8 in their second game, at Widnes. Headingley's first taste of NU rugby came on 21 September when Leeds beat Brighouse 3-0 with a Walton try.

Leigh: Gill, Anderton, Price, Wallwork, Taylor, Shovelton, Boardman, Cheetham, France, MacMasters, Pemberton, Taylor, Smith, Davies, Coop.
Leeds: Walker, Wright, H. Hainstock, Walton, Clarkson, Bastow, Midgley, Riley, Armstrong, Pickles, Gregg, Goodall, Parfitt, Hills, Fletcher.

LEEDS v. THE REST

19 April 1902   Yorkshire Senior Competition
Headingley   Referee: Mr Sedman (Liversedge)

Leeds are proud of their record of never having been relegated, but they haven't always played in Rugby League's top division. The Headingley club spent two seasons in the wilderness at the start of the twentieth century, after the fledgling professional code had been split by a breakaway of fourteen clubs. The formation of the Northern Rugby League left a host of established clubs, Leeds included, out in the cold and they were forced to enter the Yorkshire or Lancashire Senior Competitions. That was a huge blow to the Headingley men, but the positive aspect was that it led to their first ever piece of silverware. Leeds' only season in the Yorkshire Senior Competition was a magnificent triumph, as they stormed to the league title with a wonderful record of 22 wins and 2 draws from their 26 matches.

The Leeds cause was immeasurably strengthened by the demise of the Leeds parish church club, who opted to disband after the Northern Rugby League breakaway. They placed their entire playing staff at Leeds' disposal and eight players switched clubs, led by skipper George Mosley. Boosted by the influx of new talent, the Loiners breezed through their Yorkshire Senior campaign, scoring an impressive 317 points, conceding only 63, and having their try-line breached just 7 times. Leeds lost their second game of the season, at York in September, and tasted defeat again the following month at Holbeck, but after that they went on to win 19 of their remaining 20 games, the only blemish being a draw at Heckmondwike in February.

Unbeaten at home, Leeds proved themselves true champions with victory over The Rest in a special challenge match at Headingley at the end of the campaign. All rival clubs in the Senior Competition were invited to supply players for the select side to take on the champions and The Rest almost pulled off a notable victory before Leeds finished strongly to cap the best season in the club's short history. The match was played amid a mood of celebration following a meeting that week which had healed the rift between the Northern Rugby League and the clubs in the Senior Competitions. The two teams travelled to the game by charabanc from the Hotel Metropole, with a celebration dinner planned for the Headingley pavilion after the game, when the Yorkshire Senior Shield and winners' medals were to be presented.

A crowd of around 5,000 turned up for the game on a sunny afternoon, described by press reporters at the time as 'too warm for football'. Leeds turned out in white, but The Rest's players were each allowed to wear their own club's colours. With the best players in the competition on show, an exciting contest was expected, but the game itself was a disappointment. The *Yorkshire Post* reported: 'The game was pleasantly contested, though at times it seemed too much of the friendly order. The players regarded mistakes made by themselves as jokes, though there was some good football. Mosley once allowed the ball after a long kick to run clean through his legs and never attempted to cover his mistake, evidently regarding it as a huge joke. This example of indifference was not an isolated one.'

With Leeds refusing to take proceedings too seriously, The Rest's scratch side came close to pulling off a shock win. Already weakened by the withdrawal of several of their selected players, forcing them to call on last-minute replacements, they may well have held on, but for first-half injuries to Manningham duo three-quarter Lorryman and forward

Leeds 7   The Rest 5

YORKSHIRE SENIOR COMPETITION TABLE 1901–02

		P	W	D	L	F	A	Points
1.	LEEDS	26	22	2	2	317	63	46
2.	Manningham	26	19	1	6	212	65	37*
3.	Keighley	26	15	6	5	192	117	34*
4.	Wakefield Trinity	26	15	1	10	258	90	31
5.	Holbeck	26	13	6	7	138	75	30*
6.	Dewsbury	26	14	1	11	161	94	29
7.	York	26	15	1	10	187	130	29*
8.	Normanton	26	13	2	11	148	140	28
9.	Bramley	26	10	1	15	131	162	21
10.	Castleford	26	9	3	14	115	163	21
11.	Heckmondwike	26	7	3	16	83	227	17
12.	Goole	26	5	3	18	94	228	13
13.	Sowerby Bridge	26	7	0	19	65	179	12*
14.	Liversedge	26	3	0	23	67	415	6

*Two points deducted for a breach of professional rules.

Despite being omitted from the new upper echelon, Loiners hit back to win their first trophy and gain promotion. They have not been outside the top flight since.

Barker who both had to leave the field. Lorryman's accident was the most serious, as he badly twisted a knee in a tackle by Leeds half-back G. Grace. Leeds full-back J. Dean failed with an attempt to open the scoring when he missed with a drop kick, but Mosley made up for that mid-way through the first half with a sweetly-struck penalty after The Rest had been caught off-side at a scrum. Wakefield three-quarter Bennett was The Rest's best player and he produced superb tackles on Grace and T.D. Davies before almost racing in for the opening try, only to be denied by Grace's tackle. Leeds led 2-0 at half-time, but The Rest's thirteen men went ahead after the interval with a freak try. Myers, the Keighley forward, punted the ball over the heads of the Leeds defence into the arms of full-back Dean, who dropped the ball behind his own line, allowing Myers to run through and touch down. Hainsworth converted, with what The *Yorkshire Post* described as a 'pretty kick', and the select team looked capable of hanging on until three-quarter F. Mudd raced over at the corner and Mosley rounded off Leeds' triumphant season with a wonderful goal from the touchline.

At the dinner after the game, the champions were presented with their trophy and medals by Yorkshire Senior Competition president Joshua Sheldon, who happened to hold a similar role with Leeds. He told the players: 'It is a great pleasure that, after years of vicissitudes, the Leeds club has finally won something.' Replying, long-time supporter Richard Scott said: 'I have followed the team through thick and thin, but we have had more thin than thick. I trust there will now be better things in store for the Leeds club.' The gloss was taken off Leeds' triumphant season with the news that the Northern Union had decided in favour of having two divisions of eighteen clubs each for the 1902/03 campaign. Leeds were told they would only be re-admitted to the NU on condition they joined the Second Division, but the Headingley outfit overcame that disappointment in fine style, finishing as runners-up to Keighley and earning promotion to the top level, where they have remained ever since.

Leeds: Dean, Evans, Littlewood, Davies, Mudd, Mosley, Grace, Hewlett, Birch, Crumpton, McNicholas, Taylor, Crowther, Hanson, Midgley.

The Rest: Helliwell, Lorryman, Leeming, Bennett, Bland, Myers, Kelly, Voyce, Barker, Foster, Brady, Greensit, Mereweather, Holden, Hainsworth.

Leeds v. New Zealand

26 October 1907
Headingley

Tour match
Referee: W. McCutcheon (Oldham)

International fever gripped the city as A.H. Baskerville's New Zealand tourists – dubbed the 'All Golds' because of their professional status, unlike their 'All Black' Union counterparts – prepared for the sixth match of their historic visit. A crowd of 12,321, generating receipts of £455 16s 3d, flocked to Headingley for the unusual 3.30 p.m. kick-off with special half-day excursion tickets being offered by LNER from Bradford, Wakefield, Dewsbury and Batley in an attempt to entice workers who might well have been penalised for broken-time. The inaugural tourists, who were instrumental in establishing the domestic code back in Australia, having played 3 matches against New South Wales on the way out and scheduled to undertake another 10 including a three-Test series on their return, contained four 'All Blacks', including the legendary George Smith and 'Massa' Johnstone.

However, the man everyone wanted to see was the first great overseas superstar, Australian guest 'Dally' Messenger. His 'defection' was the turning point for the fledgling sport in the southern hemisphere. Widely acknowledged as the finest back in rugby, his decision to become their first professional player, as a result of the persuasiveness of Test cricketer Victor Trumper and his friend James Giltinan, ensured the tour received liberal coverage and kept the game and its 'new' rules in the public eye. That was reflected in the tourists' fees, each player receiving £150 after all expenses had been covered, except Messenger, who took £350, as agreed.

The Colonials arrived at Headingley with their reputations tarnished following a mid-week draw at Wakefield, where they received mass criticism for resorting to 'an inane kicking game which spoilt the spectacle as opposed to their usual brand of handling and running'. Captain 'Bumper' Wright and twenty-eight of his colleagues prepared the night before the game by taking a half-hour trip to the Leeds Theatre Royal *en masse*, where they sat in the stalls and made notes on the looks of nineteen young ladies who appeared on stage before them. The event was organised by the manager of Mr Melville's company, which was putting on the drama *The Ugliest Women on Earth* there at the time.

Heavy rain greeted match day, making the ground treacherous underfoot but at least washing away the fog. The tourists named their strongest line-up, and Leeds included Tom Scamans on the right wing for his debut in place of Rhodes, the Normanton flyer having impressed on trial with his speed and safe hands. He was reduced to the role of spectator in the opening stages as the Antipodeans started at a feverish pace. Fielding Birch's kick-off, the visiting forwards began a dribbling rush in the loose that took them to the Leeds line, and in the scramble that followed, William Trevarthen – who was later to sign for Huddersfield – was adjudged to have grounded the ball and was awarded a try near the posts. Messenger duly added the extras – he was to finish the tour with 146 points, over 100 more than any other player – and New Zealand had established a five-point lead in as many minutes.

The setback served only to inspire the hosts, whose ferocious tackling forced their opposition to adopt more defensive tactics which involved kicking to full-back Frank 'Bucket' Young, who ran the ball back well. The Loiners thought they had equalised when, following a scrum on the Colonials' line, Wilson found impressive centre Phil Thomas and he sent Llewellyn over, only for the referee to rule that the pass had been forward, much to the annoyance of fans who began a cacophony of booing. A mistake by Leeds three-quarter Fawcett looked as though it would give the visitors a further score, but two of them collided with each other as they attempted to pick up the ball and the chance was gone.

Leeds 2   New Zealand 8

Both teams pose for an historic picture prior to the inaugural tourists' – A.H Baskerville's 'All Golds' – match at Headingley. Kiwis George Smith and Lance Todd were to play significant roles in developing the code here both as players and administrators.

Just before half-time, Scamans broke clear for his one and only run and put in a fine cross kick, which Kiwi full-back Turtill misfielded. A try seemed certain until Messenger appeared from nowhere to scoop up the ball, finding the field from behind his own goal line to enthusiastic cheers. Even when Kiwi centre Smith dropped the ball in front of his own posts, the hosts could not capitalise, the half ending 0-5. The second half began as the first had, with the touring forwards surging to the Leeds line and being awarded a scrum. Tricky scrum-half R. Wynyard spotted a gap on the blind side and he sped over near the corner before Leeds half-back Wilson could recover his ground. Messenger narrowly missed the conversion, but again it was Leeds who responded with their pack tearing into the New Zealand forwards and the backs, led by Thomas, producing some sterling tackles as the match took on the air of a cup tie.

Several times it looked as though gaps had been carved in the visiting ranks, only for the final pass to be either too slow or go to ground, Thomas picking one such ball off his toes and, having no other option, dropping a goal. The late start meant the final quarter-hour of play took place in semi-darkness, but with a six-point lead, the tourists were able to control and dominate possession and retain their unbeaten start, with Todd outstanding. Had he seen more of the ball and had left-winger Edgar Wrigley not spurned two clear-cut chances, the margin of victory would have been greater, Leeds being the first team not to cross their try-line.

In the speeches that followed, the visitors acknowledged that although they had scored over 100 points, the strain of playing two games a week against sides desperate for their scalp was becoming greater. They noted that the intensity in the matches was far greater than when the All Blacks had visited to play Union against the amateurs two years before and that they had much to learn about the new code. The tourists returned to Headingley for the first Test, which they lost 14-6 before taking the series with victories at Chelsea and Cheltenham. Their pilgrimage here began on 9 October 1907 and ended on 15 February 1908, by which time they had played 35 matches – W 19, L 14, D 2 – and irrevocably changed the Rugby League landscape.

Leeds: Young – full-back; Scamans, Fawcett, Thomas, Llewellyn – three-quarters; Ward, Wilson – half-backs; Birch, Burnley, Harrison, Stead, Wainwright, Webster – forwards.

New Zealand: Turtill – full-back; Messenger, Smith, Wrigley – three-quarters; W. Wynyard, Todd – five-eighths; R. Wynyard – half-back; Wright, Gilchrist, Trevarthen, Cross, Byrne, Johnstone – forwards.

Leeds v. Hull

18 April 1910
Fartown, Huddersfield

Northern Union Cup final replay
Referee: J. Priestley (Salford)

Apart from reaching the Yorkshire Cup final under Union rules in 1891 – when they were beaten by Hunslet – Leeds' cup record was dreadful. In the Northern Union knock-out, instituted by the breakaway clubs in 1896/97, the Loiners had failed to get beyond the third round stage and had won only 6 out of 16 ties away from home by the time they were paired with Hull K.R. in February 1910. They had lost there in a League match a month earlier, but a committed defensive display saw Leeds hang on to record a fine 5-3 win, winger Fred Barron scoring their try. Rochdale at Headingley in the second round was poised at the same scoreline when Scottish centre C.L. Gillie scored the first of his two tries to ease the Loiners through.

Keighley's narrow Lawkholme Lane enclosure posed a difficult quarter-final hurdle, the clash becoming known as 'Bucket's match' in deference to the Herculean performance of Leeds full-back Frank 'Bucket' Young. He continually repelled the rampaging home hordes, kicked a penalty and a drop goal and put in the long-range punt which created the position for Bill Jarman to score the winning try. Such was his contribution that, on returning to Leeds railway station, he was hoisted into the street on the shoulders of jubilant fans celebrating the club's first appearance in the semi-final. There they met Warrington at Wheater's Field, Broughton, in one of the most nerve-wracking ties the competition had seen. Leeds swept into an eight-point lead, courtesy of tries by Walter Goldthorpe and Barron, but with quarter of an hour to go they were desperately hanging on by a point. The remainder of the game was played almost entirely on the Leeds line, with the Wire forwards dominating possession from a series of scrums but unable to break down an outstanding scrambling defence.

In the final, Leeds met a Hull side desperate to make up for the previous two deciders where they had been soundly beaten by Hunslet and Wakefield and had failed to score a point in either clash. With all the dignitaries and the bulk of the 19,000 crowd in place, there was no sign of the teams as the scheduled kick-off time approached. Frantic checks discovered that there was a massive hold-up on the rail network between Leeds and Huddersfield as torrential rain fell and once the protagonists had finally been ushered into Fartown, the match eventually got underway fifty minutes late. Loiners' plans were further undermined when scrum-half Jimmy Sanders was forced out of the fray by a serious injury that saw him taken home to recuperate. By then a Young penalty had given Leeds a narrow lead, but Wallace dropped a goal for the Airlie Birds and his pinpoint cross kick saw winger Cottrell race over, Rogers converting to give Hull a 7-2 interval lead.

The Leeds pack regrouped and, in a tremendous second-half effort, totally dominated the play. Jack Fawcett set up Goldthorpe for a fine individual try and although Young failed with the conversion, he put over a penalty ten minutes from time after Anderson had been caught offside. Hull winger Rogers was just bundled into touch as he went for the decisive score and Young twice attempted drop goals before just missing with a late long-range penalty, the final being drawn for the first time in the competition's history. The replay was arranged for two days later with a crowd of 11,608 attending. Both sides made two changes and a number of tactical switches – Hull losing influential skipper Anderson – with Leeds using the strong wind to their advantage with a tremendous kicking and dribbling game that pinned the East Yorkshiremen back in their own quarter. Young put over an early penalty and then dropped a spectacular goal from near halfway when fielding an E. Rogers drop-out. A spell of scrums on the Hull line saw Leeds winger H.F. Rowe go close, Webster picking up the loose ball to crash over for a try.

Leeds 26

Hull 12

The side which won the club's initial major prize, the Northern Union Cup, with a devastating display in a replay just two days after a thrilling final had been drawn for the first time in the code's history. From left to right, back row: W. Morn (trainer), W. Goldthorpe, F. Barron, H. Topham, W. Ward, W. Biggs. Middle row: J. Sanders, E. Ware, F. Webster, F. Harrison, S. Whitaker, H. Rowe. Front row: J. Fawcett, F. Young, C. Gillie, W. Jarman.

As the half drew to a close, Topham charged down a potentially relieving kick from Wallace and regathered to score, Young again converting and adding a further goal after Gillie had made the mark, leaving it 16-0 at the break. Even against the elements, such a lead seemed insurmountable, and when Goldthorpe began a move with a dribble in midfield and ghosted clear for a touchdown, Leeds were in total control. Rowe finished by the posts after Ernest Ware's superb touchline break and inside pass to Gillie, Young converting both tries into the wind to complete a faultless kicking performance that established a new record in a final, which stood until 1973.

Hull rallied, Connell and Walton grabbing scores and Rogers three goals, the respectability gained was, however, insufficient to prevent Leeds from claiming victory by a record score. There was drama towards the end of the game, first when Fawcett suffered a badly broken collar bone and then, with the crowd beginning to encroach on the playing area expecting the final whistle, the referee was called upon to admonish two of the players near the barriers. One of the frustrated Hull fans was so incensed that he charged forward, and only the intervention of touch judge Mr Kennedy from Broughton prevented him from rounding on the official. When the culprit turned his attention to the flag waver, he was knocked to the ground by Leeds prop Topham, causing a furore among those aggrieved fans nearby. The police quickly restored order and the intended assailant was led away into custody, but the referee brought proceedings to a halt with Leeds captain Webster mounting the steps proudly to collect the club's first Challenge Cup.

Leeds: Young, Rowe, Gillie, Goldthorpe, Barron, Ware, Fawcett, Webster, Harrison, Topham, Ward, Jarman, Whitaker.

Hull: E. Rogers, Cottrell, Devereux, Morton, Atkinson, Wallace, G. Rogers, Herridge, Connell, Holder, Taylor, Walton, Osbourne.

LEEDS v. COVENTRY

12 April 1913
Headingley

Northern Union
Referee: J.W. Whiteley (Wakefield)

Leeds' win over Coventry in April 1913 was unique. The Loiners ran up a then record score of 102-0 and the game remains the only occasion in the history of the thirteen-a-side code when every member of a team has got on the scoresheet. Added to that, it was and still is the highest score recorded at Headingley and the Leeds club's biggest winning margin. Popular forward Fred Webster scored eight of Leeds' twenty-four tries, then a record and a mark which has been equalled just once in blue and amber since, by the great winger Eric Harris against Bradford Northern in 1931. Remarkably, Webster managed just 76 tries in his entire 543-game career and never achieved more than seven tries in seventeen other seasons at Leeds. Under the modern Super League point-scoring system, Leeds' winning total would have been 126-0, beating by twenty points their current record tally set against Swinton Lions in February 2001.

The game was both clubs' final match of the 1912/13 season and a disappointing crowd of around 3,000 turned up at Headingley to witness history in the making. Leeds' driving force was Aussie skipper Dinny Campbell, who scored a hat-trick of tries. He was at the heart of every Loiners attack and snuffed out Coventry's only serious assault on the home line, ramming half-back Ruddick into touch in the second half. The writing was on the wall for poor Coventry by half-time when they trailed 39-0, having conceded nine tries and six conversions. But Leeds really turned up the heat in the second period, adding another thirteen touchdowns and nine more goals. Coventry arrived at Headingley with a wretched record of 25 defeats and a draw from their previous 26 games that season, and Leeds' rampage took their points against tally to 896, with just 157 for.

The visitors' abject display angered the press of the day, with the *Yorkshire Evening Post* condemning the Midlanders as 'hopeless' and claiming any attempt to keep the Northern Union game alive there would be 'absurd'. As it was, the debacle at Headingley proved Coventry's final game, the club finishing bottom of the Northern Union table and being wound up shortly afterwards. Coventry had finished twenty-third out of twenty-eight the previous year and twenty-seventh in their debut 1910/11 campaign. In their three years in the Northern Union, the Midlands side managed just 12 wins, 4 draws and 77 defeats.

Leeds' score in their final game eclipsed the previous highest Headingley total of 70-2, set against Wakefield St Austins in a Rugby Union Yorkshire Cup tie on 19 March 1892. The 102-0 scoreline exactly equalled the Northern Union record set by Ossett against Keighley in 1904. Coventry's financial plight before the game attracted sympathy from the Leeds club and spectators. The Leeds committee allowed Coventry to place collection sheets around the ground and the home faithful were encouraged to donate their spare change. If only Leeds had been as generous on the field. Other than a brief spell in the first half, Leeds refused to show their hapless visitors any mercy, keeping the Coventry line under fierce pressure with wave after wave of attacks. Thick snow in the days before the game had left the pitch in heavy condition, making running and passing difficult, and Leeds' spectators could only guess at how many points their team would have rattled up in perfect conditions.

The Leeds pack was on top from the start and it was one-way traffic right from kick-off, A. Rimmington scoring their opening try, his first and only in blue and amber, converted by C.E. Haycox. By mid-way through the second half, Campbell had embarked on a personal mission to ensure every Leeds player got on the scoresheet. J. Sutton was the last player to

---

Leeds 102   Coventry 0

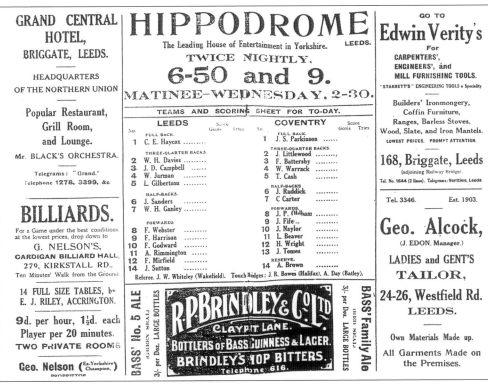

GRAND CENTRAL HOTEL, BRIGGATE, LEEDS.

HEADQUARTERS OF THE NORTHERN UNION

Popular Restaurant, Grill Room, and Lounge.

Mr. BLACK'S ORCHESTRA.

Telegrams: "Grand."
Telephone 1278, 3399, &c.

BILLIARDS.

For a Game under the best conditions at the lowest prices, drop down to
G. NELSON'S,
CARDIGAN BILLIARD HALL,
279, KIRKSTALL RD.,
Ten Minutes' Walk from the Ground.

14 FULL SIZE TABLES, by E. J. RILEY, ACCRINGTON.

9d. per hour, 1½d. each Player per 20 minutes.
TWO PRIVATE ROOMS

Geo. Nelson (Ex-Yorkshire Champion.)
PROPRIETOR

HIPPODROME
The Leading House of Entertainment in Yorkshire. LEEDS.
TWICE NIGHTLY.
6-50 and 9.
MATINEE—WEDNESDAY, 2-30.

GO TO
Edwin Verity's
For
CARPENTERS',
ENGINEERS', and
MILL FURNISHING TOOLS.
"STARRETT'S" ENGINEERING TOOLS a Speciality

Builders' Ironmongery,
Coffin Furniture,
Ranges, Barless Stoves,
Wood, Slate, and Iron Mantels.
LOWEST PRICES. PROMPT ATTENTION.

168, Briggate, Leeds
(adjoining Railway Bridge).
Tel. No. 1644 (2 lines). Telegrams: Verities, Leeds

Tel. 3346.   Est. 1903.

Geo. Alcock,
(J. EDON, Manager.)

LADIES and GENT'S
TAILOR,
24-26, Westfield Rd.
LEEDS.

Own Materials Made up.

All Garments Made on the Premises.

TEAMS AND SCORING SHEET FOR TO-DAY.

No.	LEEDS	Score Goals	Tries	No.	COVENTRY	Score Goals	Tries
	FULL BACK.				FULL BACK.		
1	C. E. Haycox			1	J. S. Parkinson		
	THREE-QUARTER BACKS.				THREE-QUARTER BACKS.		
2	W. H. Davies			2	J. Littlewood		
3	J. D. Campbell			3	F. Battersby		
4	W. Jarman			4	W. Warrack		
5	L. Gilbertson			5	T. Cash		
	HALF-BACKS.				HALF-BACKS.		
				6	J. Ruddick		
6	J. Sanders			7	C Carter		
7	W. H. Ganley				FORWARDS.		
				8	J. P. Oldham		
	FORWARDS.			9	J. Fife		
8	F. Webster			10	J. Naylor		
9	F. Harrison			11	L. Beaver		
10	F. Godward			12	H. Wright		
11	A. Rimmington			13	J. Tomes		
12	F. Mirfield				RESERVE.		
14	J. Sutton			14	A. Brown		

Referee: J. W. Whiteley (Wakefield).   Touch Judges: J. R. Bowes (Halifax), A. Day (Batley).

BASS' No. 5 ALE (GREEN SEAL) 3/- per Doz. LARGE BOTTLES

R.P. BRINDLEY & Co. LTD
CLAYPIT LANE.
BOTTLERS of BASS, GUINNESS & LAGER.
BRINDLEY'S TOP BITTERS.
Telephone 616.

3/- per Doz. LARGE BOTTLES
BASS Family Ale (RED SEAL)

Leeds produced an historic performance to trounce Coventry 102-0. This is still a record at Headingley and, uniquely, every player got on the scoresheet.

trouble the scorers. He had not kicked a goal all season and missed with two attempts before finally finding the mark to convert one of Webster's tries. Although he also crossed the whitewash himself late in the game, that remained the only goal he kicked in 67 appearances for Leeds. Webster got off the mark with the final two tries of the first half and added six more in the second period.

Webster, J. Sanders and Campbell all kicked their only goal of the season, while Rimmington and Gilbertson scored their only tries. W.H. Davies' four touchdowns took his tally for the season to 21 to top the Leeds try charts. Billy Jarman – later to earn Great Britain recognition before being killed in action in the First World War – crossed twice, and other try-scorers were Fred Godward, W.H. Ganley, Fred Harrison and Fred Mirfield, who had joined the club the previous season from Rawdon Association Football Club, despite having almost no previous experience in the handling code. Ganley, the former Leigh full-back, kicked nine goals and Haycox two before Campbell began spreading kicking duties around. The massive win brought the curtain down on a disappointing season for Leeds, who finished tenth in the table with a record of 19 wins, 1 draw and 14 defeats, more than one-fifth of their final points tally coming in the romp against Coventry.

Leeds: Haycox, W.H. Davies, Campbell, Jarman, Gilbertson, Sanders, Ganley, Webster, Harrison, Godward, Rimmington, Mirfield, Sutton.

Coventry: Parkinson, Littlewood, Battersby, Warrack, Cash, Ruddick, Carter, Oldham, Fife, Naylor, Beaver, Wright, Tomes.

Wigan v. Leeds

17 April 1915
Central Park

Championship semi-final
Referee: R. Robinson (Bradford)

Reports of Zeppelin raids on the Northumbrian coast, bombs showering Faversham in Kent and Maldon in East Anglia, heavy casualties on the Austro-Italian front and the loss of a British submarine in the Dardanelles dominated the news as Leeds qualified for the Championship play-offs for the first time in the club's history. The right of the top four clubs to contest for the title had been instituted nine years before when final league placings were decided on a percentage basis and consternation had been expressed by some clubs – most notably Huddersfield – that this was unfair. The Fartowners were undoubtedly the side of the era, Harold Wagstaff's 'team of all the talents' being virtually unbeatable as they headed the table in each of the four seasons from 1911 to 1915, losing only 14 of 136 matches in that time.

In the first two of those campaigns they took the ultimate prize but in 1913/14 Salford had beaten them 6-3 at Headingley to claim the silverware with officials of the claret and gold claiming it was a farce as they were easily the best side in the competition. Not that Leeds were complaining about the format, four wins in their last five league matches the following season seeing them finish third. By rights they should have gone to Huddersfield in the semi-final but after Rochdale sent a weakened team to Broughton Rangers and were surprisingly beaten, thereby finishing fourth, the Loiners instead travelled to Central Park with Wigan overwhelming favourites to make a fourth final, although they were yet to be victorious.

Leeds suffered a blow on the eve of the game when Test centre Albert Jenkinson, signed from Hunslet at the start of the season, was forced out suffering from quincy, Dan Lewis coming in on the wing and C.E. Haycox reverting to full-back. The sides had met two weeks before with the Riversiders running out easy winners 34-12 to give them a convincing double over the men from Headingley and Leeds had won only once before at Central Park, by a narrow margin ten years previously. One thing in Leeds' favour was the crowd, which was down to around 8,000 after Wigan's 27-2 thrashing by Huddersfield in the Challenge Cup semi-final the week before and the ease with which they were expected to win, despite being without Evans and Jenkins, although winger Miller was cleared to play after obtaining leave from his regiment in Wales. He was called upon almost immediately to repel a Leeds side that started in sensational fashion, the forwards driving deep into Wigan territory from the kick-off with an enthusiasm that knocked the hosts out of their stride. Tourist Jack Chilcott led the charge, the former Huddersfield man desperate to have a crack at his former side in the final with George Rees, Fred Webster and Billy Ward providing sterling support, especially in the scrummage.

With quality possession assured, the Leeds backs looked quicker and more direct than their counterparts, only Haycox appearing unnerved by the occasion, his usually strong kick letting him down although his catching and tackling were solid. Leeds half-backs Jimmy Sanders and Ivor Jones completely outplayed their opposite numbers and having taken an early lead, the Loiners never looked like being headed. They had already had a try disallowed for a forward pass by Dinny Campbell a yard from the home line as he fell in the tackle, when quick thinking by his centre partner Willie Davies – who picked up a dropped ball from the feet of an opponent 40 yards out – saw him outpace his pursuers to the corner, Lewis missing the conversion from wide out. Three minutes later Jones was penalised in front of his own posts 25 yards out for obstruction and Thomas kicked the penalty to make it 3-2. Wigan enjoyed their best spell; Owens elected to kick rather than pass with a two-man overlap, Willie Davies saved a try when he got back to kick the ball dead and Price knocked on with the line beckoning.

Wigan 4   Leeds 15

A shock win at Wigan in the Championship play-off was the highlight of a memorable campaign, the last full one before the First World War intervened. From left to right, back row: W. Morn (trainer), F. Webster, D. Lewis, G. Rees, J. Chilcott, F. Mirfield, W. Ward, F. Godward, B. Ward, Mr A. Townend (chairman). Middle row: F. Harrison, F. Carter, W.A. Davies, J.D. Campbell, W.H. Davies. Front row: J. Harland (assistant trainer), I. Jones, J. Sanders, M. Ashcroft.

Having weathered the barrage, Leeds broke upfield and as soon as they were in range of the posts Jones dropped a fine goal, Haycox missing a penalty soon after. Centre Curran broke away for the hosts and fed Francis and he seemed to have sent in Bradley to level the scores but the referee again adjudged the pass to have been forward. Making the most of that escape Huw Davies and Jones found space near halfway and fed Dinny Campbell for the second time in the movement, Leeds' Australian three-quarter sprinting clear for a superb score to which Lewis added the extras for an interval lead of 10-2. Three minutes after the break and the game was won, Chilcott again the provider as he set the impish Jones free, Willie Davies taking the scoring pass to go behind the posts, Lewis again on the mark with the conversion. A Thomas penalty after Leeds were caught off-side in their own quarter was all that Wigan could muster in reply, the nearest they came to a try being when winger Bradley broke clear and looked a certain scorer only for Campbell to race back and somehow knock the ball from his hands.

So convincing and dominant in all departments was the Loiners' performance, especially in the centres, that many of the crowd left long before the final whistle with some pundits even claiming that the men in blue and amber had a real chance of causing an upset against the mighty Huddersfield at Wakefield the following week. It was not to be, two tries – both from the base of the scrum – giving the league leaders a perfect start and a platform to display their astonishing skills, record-breaking winger Albert Rosenfeld relishing the space he was given as Huddersfield surpassed their previous record score in the competition winning 35-2. The following week they accounted for St Helens in the Challenge Cup by a similar score and carried off 'all four cups' in a season, emulating Hunslet in 1907/08.

Wigan: Seddon, Bradley, Curran, Price, Miller, Thomas, Owens, Seeling, Francis, Coldrick, Whitaker, Hayward, Haigh.
Leeds: Haycox, W.H. Davies, W.A. Davies, Campbell, Lewis, Jones, Sanders, Godward, Rees, Carter, Chilcott, Ward, Webster.

Dewsbury v. Leeds

26 November 1921
Thrum Hall, Halifax

Yorkshire Cup final
Referee: F. Mills (Oldham)

By the time it was scrapped in the early 1990s, the Yorkshire Cup was an unwanted and unloved competition, but in the early part of the twentieth century it was Leeds' Holy Grail. The Northern Union Yorkshire Cup was inaugurated in 1905, but by 1921 the Loiners were still waiting to win it for the first time. To say their early record in the competition was poor is an understatement. During the first thirteen years it was played – the Cup wasn't competed for during the First World War – Leeds reached the final just once, and that was a painful experience as they were crushed 24-5 by mighty Huddersfield. But at least they got there. Other years saw them beaten at the first attempt seven times, in their second game three times and the semi-final twice. Huddersfield were the dominant team during that era and they won the Yorkshire Cup six times, so when Leeds drew them in the 1921 first round, the Headingley men must have feared the worst, despite going into the game as league leaders. But two superb tries from the wonderfully named Squire Stockwell inspired Leeds to an 11-2 victory at Headingley, Halifax were vanquished 20-2 in the second round and the Loiners won 11-4 at Bramley in an all-Leeds semi-final.

Leeds' final opponents were Dewsbury, another team looking for their first Yorkshire Cup win, and the decider was staged at Halifax's Thrum Hall. The prospect of a rare taste of silverware ignited the Leeds public's imagination, much to the surprise of the railway authorities, who were caught totally off guard by the number of fans who wanted to travel to the game. The Leeds team, without injured winger Stockwell and hooker Trusler, were forced into some pre-match scrummaging practice when they had to force their way through huge crowds at Leeds Central railway station to reach their private coach. Leeds supporters made up the majority of the 15,000 crowd on a gloomy, mist-shrouded afternoon and they were treated to a thriller, but for Dewsbury the game was a case of what might have been. The Crown Flatt side had the better of the early exchanges, but they were left to rue an off-day by kicker W. Seddon and an awful injury to their former Leeds stand-off Albert Jenkinson. He had played for Leeds in the 1919 Cup final defeat by Huddersfield at Thrum Hall and it again proved an unlucky ground for him. After just 10 minutes he went down heavily and had to be carried off after treatment on the field. Doctors later discovered he had broken his right leg in two places below the knee.

With no substitutes allowed, Dewsbury were forced to play for 70 minutes with a man short and that mountain proved just too steep. Before Jenkinson's injury Dewsbury missed a chance to open the scoring when the stand-off was obstructed by Leeds' Welsh international scrum-half A. Brown, but Seddon couldn't find the target with his penalty attempt. Leeds almost made their numerical advantage tell when Syd Walmsley went close, but he was nailed just short by P. Bates. At the other end, Ward's great tackle denied Dewsbury's dangerous winger Joe Lyman before Leeds opened the scoring mid-way through the first half. Joe Brittain and Will Davies began the move and Jim Bacon finished it off, beating despairing attempted tackles by Lyman and full-back Seddon. Walmsley could not convert from wide out and Dewsbury were back in the contest moment later.

Seddon missed with a second penalty after Leeds' R. Boagey was caught off-side, but almost immediately Lyman broke away, kicked over full-back J.H. Roberts and burst Bacon's tackle to touch down a spectacular try, though again Seddon could not add the goal. Leeds went close through Brittain and then Brown broke clear, but held on to the ball too long and

Dewsbury 3

Leeds 11

The County Cup – which Leeds were to win for a record 17 times in 21 final appearances – was finally captured in 1921, although Dewsbury gave them a real fight despite losing former Loiner Albert Jenkinson who tragically broke his leg early on.

the attack was snuffed out. Five minutes before half-time, Bacon picked up a loose ball and evaded Seddon to dash over between the posts, Walmsley adding the extras. Leeds' 8-3 interval lead could have been greater, but Willie Davies was shoved into touch just short and almost immediately afterwards Hugh Davies looked certain to score from Walmsley's cross kick, but he was deceived by a wicked bounce. Seddon missed with yet another kick after Brittain was penalised for not playing the ball properly before the full-back had a lucky escape when he sent a clearing kick straight at Fred Godward, but the Leeds man knocked on. Brittain was denied by a forward pass before Willie Davies got back quickly to deny Lyman after the winger had kicked past Roberts. Leeds' poor passing and tendency to tackle too high kept Dewsbury in the game until six minutes from time, when Roberts, Bacon and Willie Davies linked to supply Hugh Davies and the Welsh winger made no mistake, out-pacing the cover to touch down by the corner flag. It was too far out for Walmsley to convert, but at 11-3 the cup was in the bag for Leeds and their long wait was finally over.

The Headingley men were aware that with Jenkinson in the Dewsbury side, it could have been a different story. His injury took some of the gloss off the Loiners' historic win and several Leeds officials took time off from the celebrations to visit the player in Halifax Infirmary, where he was awaiting surgery on his shattered leg. The Yorkshire Cup triumph was one highlight of an otherwise disappointing season for Leeds, who never recovered from a five-match losing streak in December and eventually finished fifth in the league table, missing the Championship play-offs by one place.

Leeds: Roberts, Walmsley, W.A. Davies, Bacon, W.H. Davies, Brittain, Brown, Godward, Hardaker, Gould, Boagey, Pearson, Ward.
Dewsbury: Seddon, Bates, Rees, Catterall, Joe Lyman, Jenkinson, Rogers, Craven, Dixon, Gallagher, Sharples, Birch, Leake.

LEEDS v. HULL

28 April 1923   Challenge Cup final
Belle Vue, Wakefield   Referee: F. Mills (Oldham)

As long ago as the early 1920s, Leeds had a reputation as rugby league's great under-achievers. At the start of the 1922-23 season, their meagre honours list was made up of a single triumph each in the Yorkshire League, Yorkshire Cup and Challenge Cup – and newspaper articles at the time remarked how that simply wasn't good enough for one of the game's top clubs. The lone Challenge Cup success had been against Hull in 1909-10 and that was to prove an omen for the second time Leeds lifted the trophy. The Loiners' form in the run-up to their ultimately successful Challenge Cup campaign wasn't promising, but a series of important signings underpinned improvements from around the turn of the year and a superb 11-5 first round win over Leigh at Mather Lane gave their fans genuine hope of a second appearance in the final. Leigh had been a graveyard for the hopes of many visiting Yorkshire teams, but, backed by a large and vocal travelling support which became a feature of their Cup run, Leeds rose to the task in impressive style, despite ankle deep mud which did not suit their usual style of play. Young forward G. Pickles had a try disallowed in the opening moments before W.E. Lyons touched down for the first try, though Syd Walmsley's conversion attempt hit a post. Leigh pulled two points back with a penalty goal but Leeds went into the break holding a 6-2 lead after Joe Thompson was awarded a penalty try after being shoved off a loose ball as he was about to touch down.

Injury reduced Leigh to twelve men for the whole of the second half and they never looked like getting back in the game, Arthur Binks racing over for a superb solo try from the base of a scrum, converted by Walmsley, before the hosts managed a late consolation try. Leeds hadn't had a home draw in the Challenge Cup since the war, but that ended when they were paired with Huddersfield at Headingley. A huge crowd of 34,300 turned up to see the Fartown outfit out-played in every department as the hosts romped to a 19-8 victory, thanks to two tries from Harold Buck and touchdowns by J.A. Ashton, G. Kibbler and a wonderful effort from Billy Bowen, plus two Walmsley goals. A brace of tries from Buck and two Thompson goals earned Leeds a hard-fought 10-2 win at York in the quarter-finals and a place in the last four against Barrow at Broughton, scene of their previous semi-final success thirteen years earlier.

The Loiners were hot favourites, despite a 9-4 league loss at Barrow just two months earlier, but they were lucky to avoid defeat in the first-ever drawn Challenge Cup semi-final. Setting off by rail from Central Station, with two train loads of supporters making the same trip, the Leeds players arrived in Manchester 15 minutes late due to a hold up caused by a cow which had wandered on to the line at Mytholmroyd. The delay seemed to unsettle Leeds and their fluent backs failed to develop any rhythm, while the forwards were second best to Barrow's plucky pack. Thompson missed with an early penalty attempt, but Barrow's Burgess was off-target with two similar efforts, Walmsley was twice called on to make last-gasp try saving tackles and Cumbrian winger Scott had a touchdown ruled out as Leeds were forced to defend for their lives. Leeds could have snatched an undeserved win when Jim Bacon and Joe Brittain opened up the Barrow defence in the second-half only for Buck to knock-on with the line at his mercy, but it was the Loiners who were breathing a sigh of relief at the final whistle as Burgess sent a late penalty attempt just wide.

The draw shocked the sport's authorities, who had not decided on either a replay date or venue before the initial clash. Members of the sport's ruling council opted for Halifax's

Leeds 28   Hull 3

Victory in the newly renamed Challenge Cup with Hull again the hapless victims as Jim Bacon's men run riot.

Thrum Hall, but the Challenge Cup committee then caused anger among Leeds fans and officials by changing that decision and deciding to stage the tie at Salford as a courtesy to Barrow, who faced the trickier trip from Cumbria. Both sides fielded reserve teams in league games between the semi-final and its replay less than a week later, Leeds losing narrowly to Hull and Barrow going down to Hull KR. The second game was just as tense as the first with no score in the opening period and the sides still in stalemate until the hour mark, when Leeds finally cut loose. Bill Davis (2), Ashton and Bowen all crossed for late tries and Thompson landed four goals as Leeds powered to a 20-0 win which was cruel on Barrow, but delighted the Yorkshire fans in the 9,000-strong Wednesday afternoon crowd.

As in 1910, Hull were again Leeds' opponents in the decider, after reaching the final with away victories over Broughton, Swinton and Salford and a 13-9 semi-final vanquishing of Wigan. For the first time the Cup final was staged at Wakefield's Belle Vue ground, despite complaints the stadium was too old and ramshackle for such a big occasion. Ironically, Rugby League's big showpiece in Wakefield was staged on the same day as the first FA Cup final to be played at Wembley, which must have set the handling code's administrators thinking. The authorities were hoping for the biggest crowd ever to watch a Challenge Cup final, beating the 32,596 who had seen Hull lose to Rochdale at Headingley a year earlier. New banking and crush barriers were built at the ground and the capacity was extended to 40,000, which was 11,000 more than the Belle Vue record. In the end, encouraged by reduced ticket prices as cheap as 1s 6d, 29,335 fans turned up on a beautiful April afternoon to see Leeds inflict more misery on the men from the East Riding.

Leeds: Walmsley, Buck, Bowen, Bacon, Lyons, Brittain, Binks, Trusler, Jackson, Dixon, Thompson, Davis, Ashton.
Hull: Samuel, Holdsworth, Whitty, Kennedy, Stone, Gwynne, Caswell, Oliver, Bowman, Beasty, Morgan, Taylor, Garrett.

Leeds v. Hull

Hull, whose only Cup win had come in 1914, were making a record sixth appearance in the final, which was the first all-Yorkshire affair for eight years. Leeds went into the match as slight favourites and were at full-strength after a near two-week break without a game. Hull were without Ned Rogers, the only survivor at either club from the 1910 final. He had been injured in the semi-final, along with key man Billy Batten. The Airlie Birds' 12-8 win at Headingley between Leeds' two semi-final matches had seen them finish top of the league table, but when the sides met again twelve days later at Belle Vue Leeds proved far too strong and Hull were given one of the worst beatings seen in a Challenge Cup final.

The arrival at Headingley of young former Welsh Rugby Union international Joe Thompson from Cross Keys and ex-York loose-forward J.A. Ashton had transformed Leeds' campaign and they were to the fore in a wonderful all-round display, which also featured impressive performances from their famous Busy Bees back division: Buck, Bowen, skipper Bacon, Binks and Brittain. Bacon had led Leeds out carrying their lucky black cat mascot, Felix, but there was nothing fortunate about their 28-3 triumph. Leeds' backs were too quick and their forwards too strong and from the moment Buck opened the scoring, after 22 minutes, the Loiners' name was destined to go on the Cup.

Thompson missed with two early penalty attempts before Buck had a touchdown disallowed because of a forward pass. But that was only delaying the inevitable. Binks began the first try scoring move, linking up with Brittain and Bowen, whose clever pass sent Buck racing over, with Thompson adding a simple conversion. Bacon obviously felt miffed at missing out on a hand in the opening try, as he paved the way for the second just before the break, bursting close to the Hull line before providing a neat pass to Ashton, who supplied Brittain and he sent Bowen over, Thompson's goal giving Leeds a mighty 10-point interval lead. Any thoughts of a Hull comeback were dashed early in the second-half when semi-final hero Davis, playing in the second-row, capped a magnificent individual

From left to right, back row: W. Hannan (trainer), J. Ashton, G. Jackson, J. Dixon, W. Davis, W. Trusler, J. Thompson, W. Morn (assistant trainer). Middle row: W. Bowen, S. Walmsley, J. Bacon, W. Lyons, H. Buck. Front row: J. Brittain, A. Binks.

Record signing Harold Buck, one of the five 'Busy Bees' who tormented the Hull three-quarters and claimed one of Leeds' six tries in a memorable display.

performance by snapping up a loose ball and racing over for Leeds' third converted try. A loose Hull pass allowed Brittain to cross for Leeds' fourth touchdown, with Thompson again adding the goal, and then Buck burst down the wing to send Ashton over, though Thompson's 100 per cent conversion record was broken when his goal attempt rebounded away off a post. Hull at least managed to avert a whitewash when Buck and Bowen both dropped the ball and Billy Stone snapped up possession before sending Jim Kennedy over. But fittingly, the Loiners had the last laugh as Buck and full-back Walmsley exchanged passes for the latter to touch down, Thompson landing his fifth conversion in fine style from the touchline.

Plans for a triumphant procession through Leeds had been drawn up before the game, with the team due to set-off from Thwaite Gate in Hunslet. The parade proved to be much longer than first planned as Leeds fans in cars and coaches waited outside Belle Vue for the team charabanc to emerge, before falling in line to follow the players back into the city centre in a mile-long triumphant procession. The players were met on the outskirts of the city by a brass band, who played 'See the Conquering Hero' as the team showed off the Cup to thousands of delirious supporters. Fred Webster, who had skippered the 1910 Cup winners, was present and he told reporters: 'I didn't know there were so many people in Leeds, or that they could cheer so loudly.' The Cup final triumph salvaged an otherwise disappointing campaign for Leeds. They finished eighth in the league table, with 24 wins and two draws from their 38 games, and reached the semi-finals of the Yorkshire Cup, only to be crushed 28-0 by Batley at Headingley.

Leeds v. Featherstone Rovers

24 November 1928   Yorkshire Cup final
Belle Vue, Wakefield   Referee: F. Fairhurst (Wigan)

It was billed as the 'final of contrasts' – homespun Rovers with a team gathered from within a five mile radius of their Post Office Road ground against cosmopolitan Leeds, the glamour side packed with players from five countries and two continents. It was likely that the sign-on fees for the entire Featherstone outfit amounted to less than Leeds had paid for one of their big name, classy backs: grit and determination against flair and sparkling brilliance.

Featherstone had been admitted to the professional ranks seven years before while Leeds had reached only their third Yorkshire Cup final in thirty-three years. This time the feeling was different around Headingley. The attacking prowess was clearly evident, over 300 points had been scored by the end of November, but the forwards had shown a new willingness to stand their corner in the cup rounds, especially at home to Hull K.R. in the opener. Similarly at Belle Vue and Dewsbury, the pack had shown an equal ability to mix it with their adversaries or switch tactics to make play for the speedy finishers outside them. Despite such an impressive run, Leeds were not considered favourites, Featherstone having a great record in league fixtures at Belle Vue and having disposed of a redoubtable Huddersfield outfit in their pomp at Fartown in the second round. In scrum-half Annable, the nephew of Billy Batten, and centres Hirst and Askin they had potential matchwinners and the high wind and heavy rain that accompanied the kick off was undoubtedly to their forward dominated advantage. Those conditions turned the game from a test of skill into a trial of endurance, but the above average 13,000 crowd were nonetheless treated to a contest of great drama and constant excitement.

Despite playing with the elements in their favour from the kick-off, Leeds were under the cosh for the opening quarter, the Rovers forwards keeping the ball tight and diligently maintaining possession in the Loiners half. Only the superb defensive efforts of international loose-forward Frank Gallagher, tireless scrum-half Walter Swift and the calm assurance of full-back Jim Brough, who superbly marshalled the troops in front of him, kept the line intact from the constant barrage. Brough's tackling and covering was bravery personified but his kicking was also a crucial deterrent, finding range and distance despite operating in the tightest of spaces. It was from such a breakout that the deadlock was broken in the 21st minute. Jimmy Douglas, a Scottish international forward signed a month before from Halifax, and 'Ginger' Thomas led the charge, putting pressure on Featherstone full-back S. Denton, the ball sticking in the mud as he struggled to find his feet. He had plenty of time to return the punt but unluckily failed to pick the ball up, Frank O'Rourke being the first to reach it before hacking on and claiming a touchdown close to the posts which Joe Thompson had little trouble in converting.

With a lead to defend, there was even greater determination among the Leeds pack although they were aided by the seeming reluctance of the Featherstone three-quarters to back up or move the ball swiftly when they had it in hand. In contrast, although virtually starved of possession, the Loiners made clever use of what they had, George Andrews starting a surging run with Brough, skipper Jeff Moores, Mel Rosser and finally Douglas carrying it on but just failing to find the try line. The constant defending showed in the first half penalty count, Leeds conceding twelve and receiving only two, but Jim Denton who had three long range kicks at goal failed with all of them courtesy of the vacillating wind. That dropped in intensity during the second half which allowed Leeds to gain territorial ascendancy and in their most productive attack Gallagher was again the instigator, Swift carrying on the move and setting Andrews free down the right. His superb run looked to have beaten the cover, but

Leeds 5   Featherstone 0

Jeff Moores' men were fêted throughout the city after the doughty Rovers were narrowly beaten at Belle Vue. From left to right, back row: A. Crampton, G. Rees, G. Gallagher, D. Pascoe, W. Davis, J. Douglas, A.G. Thomas, J.F. Thompson, W. Demaine, B. Heyhirst. Middle row: A.C. Lloyd, G.E. Andrews, A.F. O'Rourke, J. Moores (captain), M.A. Rosser, W.L. Desmond. Front row: W. Swift, E. Williams.

just as he seemed set to score in the corner his final stride dislodged the flag and the touchdown was ruled out.

In desperation, Featherstone mounted a final rally, Hirst getting free and finding his winger Taylor in space but his rash kick rolled dead. The final ten minutes were spent in the shadow of the Loiners' posts, Featherstone winning possession from numerous scrums but rarely looking like scoring. Their forwards Smith and Morgan had put in valiant efforts but Rovers' inability to post points in the opening half hour cost them dearly. Leeds were always the more composed side and in the few passages of open play of an enthralling match were clearly superior.

The Cup was presented by Mrs E.W. Brown, the wife of the Yorkshire President, and the Leeds players were given a tremendous reception when they returned to the city. Travelling back from Wakefield by motor coach, they were met at Thwaite Gate by the Bramley Brass Band, the procession through the city centre bringing it to a standstill. Thousands lined the route to the Griffin Hotel where the players dined with the club directors. Chairman Sir Edwin Airey thanked them for their courageous efforts in the cup run, adding that he hoped to be associated with the club for as long as he lived and that the players would look back on their days at Headingley with pleasure. Captain Jeff Moores responded, saying that he hoped they could add the other three cups as well – Leeds were denied the Championship Trophy, losing 0-2 to Huddersfield in the final game of the season. After the speeches there was another joyous parade through the streets with cheering crowds blocking the way before the players and directors capped a memorable day at the second house performance at the Empire Theatre.

Leeds: Brough, Andrews, Rosser, O'Rourke, Lloyd, Moores, Swift, Thompson, Demaine, Pascoe, Thomas, Douglas, Gallagher.
Featherstone: S. Denton, Taylor, Hirst, Askin, Whittaker, Annable, J. Denton, Barraclough, Smith, Rogerson, Shirley, Haigh, Morgan.

LEEDS v. BRADFORD NORTHERN

14 September 1931   Championship
Headingley   Referee: H. Swift

Leeds, who had ended the 1929/30 season in style with nine consecutive wins, opened the new campaign in similarly impressive, cavalier fashion. Narrow victories over York at Headingley and away to Featherstone took them to Keighley, where they inflicted the biggest home defeat seen at Lawkholme Lane, principally due to a dazzling second-half performance as the backs cut loose. Even hard-bitten locals were heard to say that it was the best footballing display ever witnessed on their home ground.

On a Monday evening two days later Bradford were hosted and although Northern were struggling – they were to finish bottom of the league for three successive seasons over the turn of the decade – their showing on the Saturday at St Helens Recreation which had seen them narrowly go down 16-7 was described as 'improved, bold and plucky'. The Loiners gave a debut to Welsh Union international forward Dai R. James from Treorchy after he had impressed in two 'A' team outings, the visitors bringing Townend onto the wing for his first start after signing him from Calder Vale and switching Shackleton from the flank to loose-forward. There were ominous signs for Bradford in the opening exchanges, Leeds' Australian Test half-back Joe 'Chimpy' Busch – playing as scrum-half in place of Les Adams – sweeping the ball wide at every opportunity and the rampant three-quarters relishing the room they were given. Chief beneficiary was compatriot winger Eric Harris who starred as the Loiners quickly built an 18-4 lead. The 'Toowoomba Ghost' had made a sensational impact in his first season the year before, almost doubling Harold Buck's tries in a season record for the club with 58 and earning his nickname for the way he imperceptibly changed pace to drift past despairing defenders.

With the home fans just beginning to sense that something special was in the offing, Bradford hit back well, forwards Malone especially and Whitaker leading the rally and winger Kitchen giving Harris a taste of his own medicine as he crossed for a brace of tries in reply showing great strength, alertness and evasion. Loiners left wing Stan Smith – a scorer in all three of the previous Championship games – also got in on the act before the break but Northern were commendably in touch, only 23-15 down at half-time. In contrast, the second period

> "**WHAT** is the match-winning secret of Toowamba's 'galloping ghost'?"
> That is how Eric Harris was once described in Brisbane, and "Bob" Scott, of Swinton, "Dick" Davies, of Halifax, and many another usually sure defender, who have been baffled and bewildered by that changing speed of the flying Leeds winger must think it an apt one.
> "Does he change his feet?"
> "How does he swerve his body at that pace?"
> These and many more questions have been asked from time to time and never more than in the spell that has elapsed since his great effort — perhaps his greatest — helped Leeds to their Cup victory over Swinton last Saturday.
> Tall, good-looking, quiet and unassuming, Harris has made himself a personality on the field on a par with that other great Colonial winger of a few years ago—Van Heerden.

Northern feel the might of ace record try poacher Eric Harris, the Aussie's eight sparkling touchdowns in this one-sided encounter equalling the club's best in a match. A eulogy after the 1932 Challenge Cup final attempts to analyse his brilliance.

Leeds 75   Bradford Northern 18

became a seemingly effortless exhibition with the crowd marvelling at the skills of Harris who was simply unstoppable every time he touched the ball, his sublime contribution preventing the contest from turning into pure farce as Leeds registered points with virtually every possession. The majority of his strikes were from long distance and whether he stayed close to the touchline or veered in-field, it seemed that the would-be tacklers melted away in front of him as his speed and swerve continually left him in acres of space.

As his try tally mounted, journalists hastily consulted the record books as the admiration for his virtuoso cameo grew. Not to be outdone Smith was equally as clinical and although he saw less of the ball he finished with a memorable hat-trick. His contribution would undoubtedly have been greater if he had not been forced from the fray with a twisted ankle. The magnificent service to the flanks was testimony to two stunning performances in the centre from Australian duo Jeff Moores and Frank O'Rourke whose instinctive interplay and speed of passing was described as 'ornamental'. Moores, who discovered and then nurtured and protected Harris' talent, was another to help himself to three tries to go with five goals while O'Rourke crowned his two touchdowns with four conversions, two of them sensational touchline efforts.

Fortunately for Bradford as the avalanche continued unabated, with Leeds registering a half century of points in the second half, the hosts were without regular goal kicker Joe Thompson who was rested, the final count of 17 tries being backed up by 12 successful place kicks. James marked a solid debut with two goals; Busch also had a kick to go with his try, but the Welshman only went on to make a handful of appearances in the blue and amber as the Headingley management tried various combinations over the season to solve a perceived scrummaging weakness. As the points mounted, great excitement centred on whether Harris would surpass Fred Webster's record match tally of eight tries for the club registered in the rout of Coventry in 1913. Unselfish work from Moores in particular ensured that his flanker closed in on the landmark, the final whistle seeing Harris equal the feat with a fifth of his eventual season's total claimed in eighty breathtaking minutes. Bradford were reduced to bit part players throughout the second forty minutes rarely touching the ball except for Coates' try near the end, the 18 points they scored ironically being the most conceded by Leeds until the end of November and second highest come the end of the campaign.

Letters to the local newspaper in the aftermath of such an emphatic win questioned the validity of the fixture, many of the correspondents wondering whether it was worth watching aside from the exceptional finishing skills shown by Harris. The performance cemented his name in the club's folklore as he went on to become the most prolific try scorer in Headingley history. In nine consecutive league fixtures from the beginning of September to the end of October 1931 he registered a staggering 20 touchdowns. Leeds' start to the campaign also set a new mark with nine successive victories, eight in the league and one in the Yorkshire Cup, their best tally for thirty years. However, the early promise tailed off after Christmas and again over Easter as the side were distracted by a highly successful Challenge Cup run.

Leeds: Brough, Harris, Moores, O'Rourke, Smith, Williams, Busch, Demaine, James, Powell, Cox, Douglas, Jenkins.

Bradford: Reed, Townend, Wood, Jones, Kitchen, Woods, Longbottom, Coates, Malone, Swan, Whitaker, Dixon, Shackleton.

LEEDS v. SWINTON

9 April 1932
Central Park, Wigan

Challenge Cup final
Referee: F. Peel (Bradford)

Leeds had to wait for their first appearance at Wembley. When the Rugby Football League took the bold decision, in 1929, to take the Challenge Cup final to the Empire Stadium, the initial plan was for a five-year trial. But in 1932 the Cup final had to be brought forward to early April because of the end of season Great Britain tour to Australia. The RFL's chosen date of 9 April coincided with an England v. Scotland soccer match at Wembley and the Football Association refused to allow the Rugby League decider to be played there the following week under an agreement with stadium authorities banning use of the pitch for up to seven days before an FA Cup final, scheduled for 23 May. To the delight of traditionalists who had opposed taking the game to the capital in the first place, the RFL eventually decided on Wigan's Central Park as a one-off venue for the 1932 Cup final. That was particularly bad luck on Swinton, who had reached the final in each of the three seasons before the move to Wembley.

The change of venue in 1932 again denied them a place beneath the Twin Towers and 70 years later they were still waiting for another appearance in the final and their first at Wembley. Ironically, the choice of Central Park as the Cup final's temporary home gave Swinton a slight psychological edge, following their 14-7 Championship final victory over Leeds there the previous season. The Cup final had seemed a long way off when Leeds were drawn away to Hull in the first round. The Loiners' Boulevard hoodoo looked about to strike again when the hosts led 2-0 deep into the second half, but a dazzling late Jeff Moores touchdown, converted by Joe Thompson, secured a famous 5-2 win. Keighley were crushed 36-2 at Headingley in the second round, Eric Harris racing in for a hat-trick of tries, and the Aussie crossed for a brace in a 21-2 home win over Leigh in the quarter-final.

The semi-final paired league leaders Leeds with Challenge Cup holders Halifax and ended in a 2-2 draw in front of a near-32,000 crowd. Four days later, two Jimmy Douglas tries and a Moores touchdown saw Leeds through to their first final in nine years with a 9-2 victory, the Loiners being boosted by the return of scrum-half Les 'Juicy' Adams. Strangely, Leeds and Halifax then met for the third time in six days in a league encounter at Headingley, but the match was abandoned early in the first half, with the game scoreless, when fire broke out in the North Stand. The stand was completely destroyed, but no one was hurt. Leeds lost three successive games after that in the run-in to the final, which was expected to be a close affair. Leeds and Swinton had each kept their try-line intact in the previous rounds and again defences were on top in the final, but it was 'Toowoomba Ghost' Eric Harris, the Loiners' greatest-ever try scorer, who was to prove the difference with the only touchdown of the game.

Leeds had a strong wind at their backs in the first half and they made it count opening up an 8-2 interval lead thanks to four penalty goals in the opening quarter by Thompson – the only survivor from Leeds' 1923 Cup final triumph – all awarded against Swinton half-back Bryn Evans for illegal feeding of the scrum. The Lancashire side's first response came on the half hour when Adams was caught off-side at the base of a scrum and Martin Hodgson landed the kick. Swinton dominated possession at the start of the second half and moved to within a converted try of the lead just four minutes after the interval when Hodgson landed his second penalty. With Swinton battering the Leeds defence, it looked as though the Cup was slipping away from the Headingley men, but a moment of brilliance turned the game on its head.

Swinton were in a great position when they won a scrum on half-way, but young centre Dick Green knocked on and the ball was snapped up by Moores. His pass found Australian centre

Leeds 11   Swinton 8

Another Eric Harris wonder try is the difference between the sides as Leeds defeat Swinton to win the Challenge Cup for the third time in a match billed as 'the contest that Wembley forgot'. Skipper Joe Thompson leads Charlie Glossop and fellow tourist John Lowe from the battle at Central Park to collect the trophy.

Frank O'Rourke, who shipped the ball on to Harris. The Aussie flier shot past Swinton's left winger Jack Kenny and found himself on half-way with only full-back Bob Scott to beat. Swinton's last line of defence moved towards the touchline to close Harris down, but was left sprawling by an electric change of pace as the Leeds winger dived over at the corner. The conversion was missed and Hodgson narrowed the gap to four points with two more penalty goals, but the Leeds defence was in no mood to let the game slip and dramatic late try-saving tackles by the excellent Adams on Evans and Evan Williams on Billo Rees – who Leeds had tried to tempt from Rugby Union a decade earlier – saw the Cup return to Headingley.

It was a magnificent achievement by Leeds, who went through their six-match Cup run without conceding a try. But campaigners hoping to see the Challenge Cup moved back up north permanently were disappointed by the attendance of just 29,000, fewer than had seen Leeds and Halifax's first game in the previous round. The following season the big game returned to Wembley and, apart from the war years, it remained there until the stadium was closed for redevelopment in 1999. The 1932 victory saw Leeds become only the fifth side to win the Challenge Cup three times and maintained their record of never having lost in the final. Wins in all five of their league games after the Cup final secured third spot in the table, but hopes of the double were dashed when the Loiners went down 9-0 at St Helens in the Championship semi-final.

Leeds: Brough, Harris, Moores, O'Rourke, Goulthorpe, Williams, Adams, Thompson, Lowe, R. Smith, Cox, Douglas, Glossop.

Swinton: Scott, Buckingham, Green, H. Evans, Kenny, Rees, B. Evans, Strong, Armitt, Wright, Hodgson, Beswick, Butters.

LEEDS v. WAKEFIELD TRINITY

27 October 1934
Crown Flatt, Dewsbury

Yorkshire Cup final
Referee: P. Cowell (Warrington)

Leeds v. Wakefield Trinity
Yorkshire Cup final replay
Fartown, Huddersfield
31 October 1934

Leeds v. Wakefield Trinity
Yorkshire Cup final second replay
Parkside, Hunslet
7 November 1934

The Loiners' 1934 Yorkshire Cup final meeting with Wakefield Trinity wasn't so much a game as a saga. Getting there was just the half of it for Leeds who cruised through three games into the final and then had to play as many again before finally lifting the famous trophy for the fifth time. When Leeds drew with Wakefield in the final at Dewsbury's Crown Flatt, it was the first Yorkshire Cup decider in the competition's 27-season history to finish all square. The sides couldn't be split in the replay four days later at Fartown and it needed a second replay, this time at Hunslet's Parkside ground, to finally settle the issue. The Loiners made an impressive start to the 1934/35 campaign, losing just one of their opening 16 league fixtures, a sequence which included 10 straight wins. Sandwiched in the middle of that successful spell was a Yorkshire Cup run which, aided by three home draws, saw off Bramley, Hull and Halifax, the red-hot Loiners scoring 74 points in the process and conceding just 14.

What was expected to be the competition decider was the first major final staged at Crown Flatt and 22,598 crammed into the ground to see it. Leeds suffered a blow before the game when star Aussie Chimpy Busch was ruled out through injury, J. Fawcett taking his place at scrum-half. Problems deepened for the Loiners when they lost the toss and were forced to play uphill against a gale-force wind in the first half and then to make matters worse they were reduced to 12 men on the half hour when centre Gwyn Parker had to leave the field with concussion. By that stage Leeds were 5-0 down, Trinity scoring the only points of the opening period when a lovely run by A. Pickard created a fine try for A. Burrows, with Ernest Pollard adding the conversion. The wind at Leeds' backs made up for their numerical disadvantage in the second-half and they levelled when Pickard and Burrows, who had created Trinity's score, turned from heroes to villains, colliding going for the ball at the base of a scrum and allowing Ken Jubb to scoop up and cross in the corner, Jim Brough landing an incredible touchline conversion to complete the scoring in a 5-5 draw.

Leeds made two changes to their side for the replay, Sep Aspinall, who had been suspended for the first match, taking over at loose-forward from Iowerth Jones, with Busch returning to replace Fawcett. Wakefield brought in R Moore at centre and, with Pickard injured, Pollard moved to stand-off with Burrows taking over at scrum-half. In front of a 10,300 crowd, Trinity scored the only points of the first half when Pollard stroked over a 40th minute penalty – and for a long spell it looked as though that would be enough to win them the cup, only for Leeds to snatch another replay in an incredible finale. Leeds failed to make any impression on a determined Trinity defence for the first 30 minutes of the second period, but they threw everything into attack in the final 10 with Len Higson knocking on as he tried to reach over and Eric Harris being denied by full-back Gordon Bonner at the corner. With four minutes to go, Leeds had what looked like being their final chance when they were awarded a penalty well to the side of the Wakefield posts, but Brough hit an upright with his angled kick and the rebound went to ground to force a scrum. Wakefield won the heel and the ball was slipped to Bonner, who attempted to clear downfield only for Dicky Ralph to collect the kick and equalize the

Leeds 5	Wakefield Trinity 5
Leeds 2	Wakefield Trinity 2 (replay)
Leeds 13	Wakefield Trinity 0 (second replay)

scores with a dramatic last-ditch drop goal. The second replay attracted a crowd of 19,304 to see Leeds make it third time lucky. After being on the back foot for most of the two previous games, the Loiners were in control throughout as winger Stan Smith terrorised his former club.

Leeds took the lead for the first time in the three encounters on 20 minutes through a Brough penalty and then on the stroke of half-time Aspinall, now playing in the second-row, hurled out a wide pass to Smith, who touched down at the corner for an unconverted try. Leeds were again reduced to twelve men moments after the break when Higson went off with damaged ribs, but there was no way back for Trinity who could not find gaps in the Leeds defence. The Loiners increased their lead in spectacular style when a passing move sent Stan Brogden away and he drew full-back Bonner before whipping out a perfect pass to Smith, who crossed untouched. Moments later Ralph and Parker linked up to give Smith his hat-trick, Brough completing a 13-0 win with the conversion. Smith, who had notched a hat-trick in the opening win over Bramley, thus completed the feat of being among the try-scorers in each round of the competition, though he had failed to cross the whitewash in the first two legs

WORTHY WINNERS AT THIRD ATTEMPT

Superiority of Speed Demonstrated

TRINITY'S GOOD FIGHT

By Our Rugby League Representative
PARKSIDE, Wednesday

It was, of course, entirely fitting that when the referee's whistle sounded here this afternoon for the last time in this prolonged Cup final, the trophy, the cause of all the bother—the cause of 240 minutes' exciting football—should be duly and ceremoniously presented to Jim Brough, the Leeds captain, by Mr. W. Jackson, the vice-chairman of the Yorkshire County Union.

of the final. Things went downhill for Leeds after the high of their eventual Yorkshire Cup triumph. After leading the league table on Christmas Day, they slipped to a fifth-place finish, although they did add the Yorkshire League Championship to their county cup success.

Replay
Leeds: Brough, Harris, Brogden, Parker, S. Smith, Ralph, Busch, Higson, Lowe, Satterthwaite, Jubb, Dyer, Aspinall.
Wakefield Trinity: Bonner, Farrar, F. Smith, Moore, Smart, Pollard, Burrows, Wilkinson, Field, Hobson, Horton, Exley, Rowan.

Referee: P. Cowell (Warrington)

Second replay
Leeds: Brough, Harris, Brogden, Parker, S. Smith, Ralph, Busch, Higson, Lowe, Satterthwaite, Jubb, Aspinall, Jones.
Wakefield Trinity: Bonner, Moore, F. Smith, Pollard, Smart, Burrows, Pickard, Wilkinson, Field, Hobson, Horton, Exley, Rowan.

Referee: J. Orford (St Helens)

Leeds: Brough, Harris, Brogden, Parker, S. Smith, Ralph, Fawcett, Higson, Lowe, Satterthwaite, Dyer, Jubb, Jones.
Wakefield Trinity: Bonner, Farrar, F. Smith, Pollard, Smart, Burrows, Pickard, Wilkinson, Field, Hobson, Horton, Exley, Rowan.

LEEDS v. WARRINGTON

18 April 1936   Challenge Cup final
Wembley   Referee: Mr A.S. Dobson (Featherstone)

A low-key start on the 1936 Challenge Cup trail gave little indication of the drama or history that was to follow. It began with a hard fought home win over lowly Dewsbury, who were ahead by seven unanswered points when their speedy winger Hobson was somewhat harshly banished from the fray by Wigan referee Mr Timility prior to half-time. The understrength visitors were only a point behind with barely three minutes to go, but late tries to Eric Harris and Aubery Casewell eased the Loiners through. Harris landed conversions to both of the scores, two of only 16 goals he kicked for the club during his eight glorious years there.

Expectations were hardly raised after the second round with a perfunctory win at Streatham and Mitcham by 13-3, although the tie was played in atrocious wet conditions which negated any hope of running rugby. Nevertheless, a fortnight later, Leeds produced one of their greatest ever knockout performances in the quarter-finals. Drawn at the seemingly impregnable Boulevard, an exceptional, desperate rearguard action in front of a massive crowd in the most hostile and combustible of environments saw the gallant Loiners hold out for an unlikely victory. A record 28,798 passionate fans crowded onto the very edge of the playing arena, which itself resembled a mudbath, to see invincible league leaders Hull stunned as heroic cover defence ably led by stand-in full-back Charlie Eaton repelled their almost constant waves of attack. In the most tense and dramatic of second halves and with the score level at 2-2, a sensational tackle by scrum-half Evan Williams to deny home winger Gouldstone a seemingly certain try turned the volatile contest. Leeds second-rower Ken Jubb led the breakout, Gwyn Parker was the vital link and Fred Harris' trademark dummy scissors saw him streak down the touchline and gloriously in at the corner. Missed penalties and drop goals, disallowed tries and two home sendings off wrecked the Airlie Birds' desperate bid for salvation as the agitation of their incensed, fanatical backers reached fever pitch, play being halted on several occasions as the fans cascaded onto the playing surface. Eventual defeat was Hull's first in eighteen months at the Boulevard and only their second in sixty league and cup matches there.

It may have felt like a final for the men from Headingley, but their nemesis stood in the way of a first ever trip to the Twin Towers in the shape of Huddersfield, another ground record crowd of just under 38,000 packing Wakefield's Belle Vue to witness an epic semi-final. This time on a perfect surface, both sides endeavoured to play fast, open rugby, contemporary reports noting that there were, 'passages of sustained brilliance in which attack was countered by attack with the ball being whirled from one end of the field to the other and back again, and with the pace such that it seemed impossible for the best trained man to stand it'. Ultimately, the greater speed of the Leeds three-quarters was crucial, allowing them to cover the bewildering forays of the Fartown backs, prompted by outstanding scrum-half Pepperell. In response, Loiners' finishing was absolutely clinical. That was again down to voracious winger Eric Harris, whose initial score after more wondrous dexterity and acceleration from namesake Fred, cancelled out Alec Fiddes' excellent effort in the first half. Eric's uncanny eye for the gap then caught the Huddersfield defence off guard as he sped over for his brace just after the break to secure a memorable and exalted victory.

Thousands of Leeds fans made the pilgrimage to north London by charabanc and special trains for the final against a full strength and highly fancied Warrington outfit who had themselves lost to Huddersfield at the Empire Stadium three years earlier and were making a record eighth appearance in the decider. For the third consecutive tie, a new attendance

---

Leeds 18   Warrington 2

A first visit to the Twin Towers saw Leeds easily overcome Warrington after Iowerth Isaac's controversial early try had given them the advantage. From left to right, back row: Isaac, Hall, Dyer, Eric Harris, Casewell, Jubb. Front row: Satterthwaite, Williams, Ralph, Brogden, Fred Harris, Eaton, Parker. Inset: Smith, Brough, Whitehead.

mark was established, with 51,250 settling on the terraces to welcome the sides, beating the previous best by almost ten thousand and producing the highest receipts of £7,200. Leeds played in their change shirts of amber with blue collar and cuffs so as not to clash with Wire's traditional primrose and blue, but were without Great Britain winger Stan Smith who was still suffering from a long term leg injury. Stan Brogden moved onto the left flank and Parker – whose tackle on Prosser in the semi-final had been a game saver – again came in at centre.

Significantly, the Loiners were boosted by the return of urbane skipper Jim Brough who led out his side into the blazing sunshine alongside opposing custodian, esteemed Aussie Bill Shankland. Their respective performances summed up the match, Brough was impeccable from the kick-off, his pinpoint kicking as he prolonged their duels a constant torment, leaving his adversary mentally drained and physically exhausted by the close. His tackling was tenacious and stifling and his support play sublime in a performance which would have easily won the man of the match nomination had the award existed. Leeds wrested the initiative in the early stages and never looked like losing control with Brough's expert marshalling and cajoling of his pack ensuring that they hassled and harried the much vaunted Warrington six into mistakes and submission while the fastest three-quarters in the game relished the open spaces on offer, thus confirming the growing belief that it was forwards who took a side to Wembley but backs which won the trophy.

Leeds: Brough, E. Harris, F. Harris, Parker, Brogden, Ralph, Williams, Satterthwaite, Hall, Dyer, Jubb, Casewell, Isaac.

Warrington: Shankland, Garrett, Hawker, Dinsdale, Jenkins, Newcomb, Goodall, Hardman, Cotton, Miller, Flannery, Arkwright, Chadwick.

LEEDS v. WARRINGTON

Such was the Yorkshiremen's dominance that the match was never really allowed to develop into a true contest. Warrington never recovered from conceding an early score, which was tinged with controversy. In the seventh minute Eric Harris worked himself free of his marker on the right and as the cover converged waiting for his trademark acceleration on the outside, he surprised them all by cross kicking for unmarked Iowerth Isaac to gather and romp over on the opposite wing. The Warrington defenders were convinced that the loose-forward was in an offside position but, despite their protests, referee Albert Dobson from Featherstone was adamant that the try was legitimate. Harris having continued his run down the touchline to play him on side, Evan Williams converted to make it 5-0.

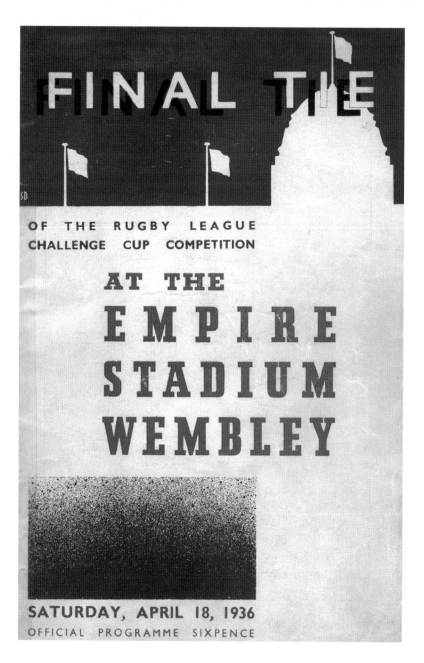

FINAL TIE

OF THE RUGBY LEAGUE
CHALLENGE CUP COMPETITION

AT THE

EMPIRE
STADIUM
WEMBLEY

SATURDAY, APRIL 18, 1936
OFFICIAL PROGRAMME SIXPENCE

Arriving back home after beating Acton and Wilsden on the following Monday, victorious captain and acknowledged man of the match Jim Brough and his team are met off the train by the Lord Mayor of Leeds.

Wire never established a rhythm following that setback, despite monopolising possession: they were to win 46 of the afternoon's 64 scrummages in total. Hawker knocked on after a Jenkins kick had spiralled away from the Leeds defence and Garrett did likewise when it appeared that the line was at his mercy as Warrington attacked down the right, a fine Shankland penalty from near half-way after a Fred Harris foul being all they could muster in reply. Brough completely dominated the pace and tempo of the game with his imperious raking kicks or graceful darts and just before the half hour Leeds conjured a magnificent try to effectively settle the contest. It went to centre Fred Harris as his majestic dummy scissors routine again worked to perfection. Collecting the ball in midfield, he shaped as if to link up with Eric Harris and as the winger moved inside to confuse the defence, Fred held on to the ball, shot down the touchline, chipped over the hapless Shankland as he approached and regathered on the full to claim a picture score. Williams added a 38th minute penalty to give Leeds a commanding 10-2 interval lead and the second half was one-way traffic.

Loiners added two more tries, the first being described as one of the best individual efforts ever witnessed at the famous venue. Eric Harris had threatened to unleash his sensational acceleration all afternoon and the wait proved worthwhile as he shot inside three bemused would-be tacklers, kicked over a further two as they desperately thought that they had reached him, gloriously won the race to the ball and then somehow twisted his way over the line for a truly memorable solo touchdown which Williams converted.

With the Warrington defence in disarray, Parker made the most of his opportunity, spotting a gap at acting-half and scything and dummying his way to the whitewash to cap a brilliant display which was generally regarded as being his best in the famous colours. The final scoreline of 18-2 was the widest margin seen at Wembley and a delighted Brough deservedly mounted the famous steps to collect the trophy from Lord Derby, Leeds equalling Huddersfield's record of four wins. The highlight of his side's jubilant lap of honour came when he jumped on top of the greyhound traps behind the goal in front of a party of 1,600 children from the Leeds and Hunslet schools association who had undertaken the journey of a lifetime to witness the lifting of the glittering silver prize.

The team's huge civic reception – with Lord Mayor Alderman Leigh and the pipe band of the Yorkshire Jocks greeting the returning heroes at the central railway station – was delayed as Leeds remained down south to complete their penultimate league fixture at Acton and Willsden on the Monday, their third different venue of the campaign in the capital. The day before they had met up with their vanquished Wembley opponents for a commemorative lunch at Windsor. The Acton match was notable for Eric Harris grabbing seven tries in a 54-4 win and thereby creating a new total for touchdowns in a season, his tally of 63 still being a club record. Among that number included an incredible haul and unparalleled sequence of 36 tries in 17 consecutive matches, a run that was ironically brought to an end in the terrific cup battle at the Boulevard.

LEEDS v. HUNSLET

30 April 1938
Elland Road, Leeds

Championship final
Referee: F. Fairhurst (Wigan)

The 1938 Championship final was probably the most famous game of rugby league ever staged in Leeds and certainly the most eagerly awaited. Ever since the early days of the Northern Union, fans of Leeds and Hunslet had dreamed of their sides meeting in a major final. Leeds and Hunslet both qualified for the Championship semi-finals in 1928 and 1932, only to lose out, but in 1938 the sport's best two teams both came from Leeds and the dream final was a reality at last. Hunslet topped the table at the end of the regular league season with a record of 25 wins and three draws from their 36 matches and Leeds were second, just a point behind with 25 wins and two draws.

Hunslet beat Barrow 13-7 in a nervy semi-final at Parkside and when the Loiners took on Swinton two days later, members of the Hunslet team were in the 29,000 Headingley crowd to see if their arch-rivals could set up the all-Leeds title decider. Under-strength Leeds, missing seven first-choice players, trailed 2-0 at half-time and were still behind going into the final quarter, only for Eric Harris to intercept a pass near his own line and race clear for a sensational try, converted by Evan Williams to seal a nerve-tingling 5-2 triumph.

The Championship decider was originally due to be staged at Wakefield's Belle Vue ground, but at the request of officials from both finalists it was switched to Leeds United's Elland Road stadium to become the first game of rugby played there for almost forty years. Hunslet were looking for their second Championship, after beating Oldham following a replay way back in 1908. For Leeds, it was their fifth Championship final, their third of the decade, and they were yet to taste victory. The tie put the city's newspaper, the *Yorkshire Evening Post*, in a difficult situation and its sports writers were desperate to appear impartial, taking the attitude of 'we don't care who wins as long as it's a good game'. On the day of the match the newspaper predicted the Loiners had 'an even chance, no more than that' – though Leeds' injury crisis made Hunslet most people's slight favourites.

The all-Leeds final created massive interest on both sides of the river and the decision to take the game to Elland Road was vindicated by a huge crowd of 54,112, still the biggest for a game of rugby league in the city. Ironically, they had to make a swift exit after the game as Leeds United had arranged a reserve match for the same evening. Magistrates allowed pubs near Elland Road to open half an hour early and thirty buses were laid on to ferry fans from City Square to the ground from two hours before kick-off. Queues formed at the boys' entrance before the turnstiles opened at 1pm and there were crowds of people milling around outside before even the teams arrived. Some fans climbed on to the stand roof in an attempt to gain a better view of the action, but they were chased down by constables and by kick-off the gates were closed with many supporters locked outside.

For all its dramatic build-up, the game itself was a disappointment and full-strength Hunslet were more convincing winners than the final 8-2 scoreline suggested. Leeds went into the final without forwards Ken Jubb and Alf Watson, who were both suspended, and were also missing the injured Cliff Whitehead, plus backs Cliff Evans, Fred Harris and Jim Brough. The good news for the Loiners was the return of inspirational Australian stand-off Vic Hey, who had missed the semi-final through injury. That proved a false dawn though as Hey picked up a new knock and he and winger Stan Smith, who was injured mid-way through the first-half, were both reduced to the role of passengers. The injuries gave Leeds fans an excuse in the pubs and workplaces after the game, but Hunslet were already on top by the time

Leeds 2

Hunslet 8

The greatest sporting event to capture the imagination of the city as 54,112 fans crowd into Elland Road for the parochial Championship final. Leeds winger Stan Smith is halted by Hunslet's Eric Batten and Cyril Morrell.

Smith and Hey were injured. The Parksiders' forwards dominated the Leeds six and, inspired by the splendid form of centre Cyril Morrell and stand-off Oliver Morris, their backs had the class to open up the Loiners' over-stretched defence. Leeds drew first blood on seven minutes when – after Hunslet's Jack Walkington had failed with a penalty kick into the strong wind – the Parksiders were caught offside and Ted Tattersfield landed a well-struck goal to give the Headingley men a two-point lead.

The result could have been different had Leeds made the most of a brief numerical advantage while Hunslet prop Mark Tolson was off the field receiving treatment to a leg injury, but Evan Williams twice failed to find Eric Harris with what could have been try-scoring passes and a Hey break was wasted through lack of support. Tolson's return inspired Hunslet and they grabbed the opening try when centre Ernest Winter stepped and dummied his way over, only for Walkington's conversion attempt to hit a post and bounce out. That was on 23 minutes and Leeds were opened up again six later when, after Walkington had again been off-target with a penalty shot, Winter broke away to send Irish winger Jimmy O'Sullivan over by the flag for an unconverted try. Playing into the wind and with injuries beginning to bite, Leeds never really looked like pulling the game out of the fire in the second-half. After Tattersfield missed with an early penalty attempt, the Loiners had just two clear try-scoring opportunities, Harris being shoved into touch after a Dai Jenkins break before the scrum-half raced away, but couldn't find Stan Brogden with his pass. Walkington's field kicking kept Leeds on the back foot and he sealed Hunslet's title late on with a long-range drop goal.

Leeds: Eaton, E. Harris, Williams, Brogden, Smith, Hey, Jenkins, Satterthwaite, Murphy, Prosser, Tattersfield, Dyer, Duffy.
Hunslet: Walkington, Batten, Morrell, Winter, O'Sullivan, Morris, Thornton, Tolson, White, Bennett, Newbound, Stansfield, Plenderleith.

LEEDS v. SALFORD

24 December 1938
Headingley

League match
Referee: F. Fairhurst (Wigan)

Headingley's world famous cricket ground has staged club, county and Test matches for more than a century, but only once has it played host to Rugby League. On Christmas Eve 1938, freak weather conditions saw Headingley's rugby arena frozen solid, while the cricket pitch remained soft, lush and well-grassed. With mighty Salford, third-placed in the league and known throughout the north of England as the Red Devils, due to visit for a vital game as part of a hectic Christmas programme which also had matches scheduled for Boxing Day and 27 December, the Leeds management decided the show must go on.

The final pre-war winter was a harsh one and the days leading up to Christmas Eve produced frost followed by snow, followed by a thaw and then more frost, with many sports matches falling victim to the extreme conditions. The Leeds authorities were determined to avoid a fixture backlog and desperate not to miss out on a big holiday gate. The Headingley groundstaff were confident they could get the football field ready for the big match, but plans were also put in place for play to be switched over to the cricket pitch and when the rugby arena failed an inspection on the morning of the game, a major operation swung into action. Forty men were brought in to clear snow from the cricket pitch and remove straw which had been laid as a precaution. A playing area measuring 106 yards in length by 75 wide was marked out, the maximum width and only four yards short of full length. Terracing at the ginnel side of the cricket arena and the Kirkstall Lane end were made ready for spectators and the capacity was estimated at around 25,000. The pitch ran from the new North Stand to the Kirkstall Lane end, trespassing on the cricket wicket, but the turf was in excellent condition and the scene was set for a genuine battle of the giants. All the Headingley staff's hard work paid off as a crowd of between 12 and 15,000 fans flooded through the turnstiles for a truly unique and historic occasion – and they were rewarded with a superb, free-flowing encounter.

Leeds were in a re-building phase as the successful side of the mid-1930s broke up. Their new-look team had surpassed expectations but, though Leeds led the table after a run of just one defeat in 17 games, Salford went into the match as slight favourites, buoyed up by a magnificent defence which had conceded only a dozen tries in 20 League and Lancashire Cup matches that season. The players entered the field down the same path from the pavilion used by countless famous cricketers and Leeds began the unique match defending the Kirkstall Lane End. Salford had identified Australian Vic Hey as the Loiners' dangerman and their fears proved justified as the former Kangaroo stand-off became the first and only man to score a try on Headingley's cricket field. The honour of grabbing the first rugby points went to former Bramley Old Boys Rugby Union full-back Jack Kelly, who landed a first-half penalty goal after missing with a similar effort early in the game.

Hey, one of the finest players ever to wear the No. 6 jersey for Leeds, was in the thick of the action at both ends of the field, first producing a last-gasp try-saving tackle to deny Salford winger Barney Hudson, before bursting on to a pass from half-back partner Dai Jenkins, only to be dragged down a yard short of the line as Salford's defence lived up to their mighty reputation. Hey's historic try came late in the opening period, when Welsh scrum-half Jenkins broke clear and slipped back a clever pass to the Aussie, who swerved and side-stepped through the normally impregnable Salford defence. Kelly failed to add the extras, but Leeds went into the break with a 5-0 advantage, although they were fortunate that Salford's

Leeds 5   Salford 0

The only man to score a try on the equally famous Headingley cricket ground, Australian international and later renowned Kangaroo coach Vic Hey. Although he played in only six Test matches from 1933 to 1936 before he left to join Leeds, he is still rated as one of the finest stand-offs the Aussies have ever produced.

Gus Risman had failed to pack his kicking boots. He missed three penalties in the first half and went on to fail with two more attempts in a scoreless second period. It was Leeds who had to do most of the defending after the interval, with Risman and fellow centre Alan Edwards going agonisingly close to getting the visitors back on level terms, only to be denied by the Loiners' never-say-die defence. The experiment of moving the game to the rugby pitch was hailed as a huge success, but was never repeated, although the Leeds management's innovative reputation continued in the 1960s, when Headingley's rugby ground became only the second sports pitch in the country, after Scottish Rugby Union's Murrayfield head-quarters, to have under-soil heating installed. Salford's record later that season underlined the quality of Leeds' Christmas Eve win.

The men from the Willows went on to finish top of the table, with just 7 defeats and 3 draws from their 40 games, before claiming their third Championship of the decade with an 8-6 win over Castleford in the final at Maine Road. They also became the first side to reach Wembley in successive seasons, only for their hopes of retaining the Challenge Cup to be dashed in a heavy defeat by Halifax, who had pipped Leeds in the semi-final. The Christmas Eve victory kicked off a successful festive period for the Loiners, who went on to beat Wakefield Trinity on Boxing Day and Batley 24 hours later, when ex-Llanelli Rugby Union centre Gareth Price made his debut, all without conceding a try. That extended their unbeaten run to 12 games and by New Year's Eve, an October defeat at Warrington remained Leeds' only league set-back. But the fateful year of 1939 began with defeat at Halifax on 2 January and though Leeds led the league until the end of that month, they eventually slipped to a disappointing fifth spot, missing out by one place on the Championship play-offs.

Leeds: Kelly, E. Harris, F. Harris, Evans, Smith, Hey, Jenkins, Prosser, Murphy, Wheatley, Dyer, Jubb, Tattersfield.
Salford: Osbaldestin, Hudson, Miller, Risman, Edwards, Gear, Watkins, Davies, Day, Bradbury, Dalton, Thomas, Feetham.

LEEDS v. HALIFAX

6 June 1942
Odsal, Bradford

Challenge Cup final
Referee: P. Cowell (Warrington)

Bill Shankly's often quoted assertion that 'Some people think football is a matter of life and death. I can assure them it is much more serious than that', is a sentiment that anyone passionate about their sport or club can relate to, not least Rugby League fans. Occasionally, however, results hardly matter and in the case of wartime rugby, merely the fact that there was a form of entertainment for a beleaguered public to watch and follow was enough of a tonic, not that the players ever gave anything less than their very best.

League competition was suspended for a month after the outbreak of hostilities in September 1939, the wartime Emergency League being regionalised for the first two seasons and then combined as sides dipped in and out subject to their available resources. Guest players were allowed – Leeds' roster over the war years averaged around 70 players a season – and those back on leave were given rapturous receptions whenever they donned their boots, with the title being decided on a percentage basis of fixtures completed. After suspending the Challenge Cup for a season – unlike during the First World War, when mass enlistment saw it shelved between 1915 and 1919 – it was brought back in 1941 as an end-of-season event which offered a more realistic chance of success.

War savings certificates replaced medals for the finalists with the winners receiving four and the losers three. Twenty-one clubs entered, with Leeds among eleven receiving byes to the second round. Narrow victories at Dewsbury and a thrilling derby at Hunslet took them into the semi-finals, which were made into two-legged ties such was the interest generated. Although Headingley's capacity had been initially reduced to 8,000 by the Home Office in case of air raids, double that number witnessed the home encounter with Bradford which ended in a draw, Leeds qualifying for the final back at Odsal with a 12-2 success inspired by Eric Batten, who was on loan from Hunslet. In the decider, Halifax were the opponents with nearly 29,000 fans witnessing a dominant second-half performance by the Loiners who secured a 19-2 success courtesy of a brace of touchdowns each to the left-sided pairing of Vic Hey and Wigan guest Johnny Lawrenson. The Cup gave provided a deserved spotlight for some of that era's unsung heroes, none more so than Loiners' electrifying stand-off Oliver Morris. The supremely gifted Welshman from Pontypridd initially moved to the city to play for Hunslet before crossing the River Aire just prior to the outbreak of war, his flashes of brilliance in partnership with Dai Jenkins lightening the general gloom and accounting for the first try in the 1941 final. The pair were in harness the following season when eighteen clubs entered, all the cup rounds having been made two legged contests.

After Leeds were initially handed a bye, Wakefield were beaten 8-3 on aggregate – avenging a Yorkshire Cup elimination over the same format – and Hull were easily vanquished thanks to an excellent home display, with Stan Satterthwaite and Vic Hey again outstanding, in the third round. Oldham were unable to prevent Leeds from a second successive Odsal final appearance with Halifax again providing the opposition – this was only the second time in 41 years that the same teams had met in consecutive deciders. Leeds were strengthened by the surprise return of 38-year-old Jim Brough from South Africa. He had been their captain when they had lifted the trophy for the first time at Wembley in 1936, the year he also captained the Lions tourists Down Under. For eighty minutes he rolled back the clock to produce a performance of stunning virtuosity and class, dominating the Halifax backs with a majestic short and long kicking game, fielding all of their punts effortlessly and

Leeds 15   Halifax 10

Try scorer Oliver Morris looked set to be one of the greatest half-backs to don the blue and amber when he arrived at Headingley from Hunslet on the eve of the Second World War. Tragically, he was to die in the conflict just two years later.

providing the telling link for a star-studded three-quarter line which included Salford's Test men Gus Risman and Alan Edwards who opened the scoring in the early minutes when he raced onto Morris' crosskick wide on the right.

Halifax's pack, marshalled by Test man Tommy McCue (on loan from Widnes) and led by prop Chris Brereton, who was to come to Headingley in 1946, and Harry Millington (also Widnes) tried to stem the flow. However, the Leeds six ensured sufficient possession for their lightning backs to inflict maximum damage, with Dai Prosser, Frank Gregory – the wrestler from Warrington – and George Brown (Batley) excelling. Jenkins re-paid Morris for the year before when he turned provider, jinking clear with sparkling footwork before putting a precision grubber for the eager stand-off to race onto and outstrip the cover to the line. Halifax full-back Hubert Lockwood kept his side in touch with three penalties, but the Loiners' advantage would have been greater had Hey, who had been outstanding in the early rounds, not been a virtual passenger on the wing after straining a leg muscle only 15 minutes in. Just before the break a mistake by the Thrum Hallers as they brought the ball out of defence saw Edwards swoop for the third touchdown, Risman's conversion making it 11-6.

Few among the 15,250 bemoaned the fact that there were limited try-scoring chances in the second half, Satterthwaite ensuring that the Leeds line would not be breached as he marshalled the cover superbly and twice Brough carved out golden opportunities, only for the scoring pass to go astray before an understandable mix up between the unfamiliar backline saw them overrun the ball. The scoring was restricted to a brace of successful penalties to each side, Leeds claiming the spoils 15-10 and keeping their line intact much to the acclaim of their fans, who had witnessed a record-breaking sixth win out of six in the competition. For all their jubilation, the result and the sport was put into perspective two years later when news reached West Yorkshire that Morris had tragically paid the supreme sacrifice when he was killed in action in northern Italy.

Leeds: Brough, Edwards (Salford), Risman (Salford), Hey, Evans, Morris, Jenkins, Morris, Jenkins, Prosser, Murphy, Satterthwaite, Gregory (Warrington), Brown (Batley), Tattersfield.
Halifax: Lockwood, Bevan, Smith, Rule, Doyle, Todd, McCue (Widnes), Brereton, Jones (Widnes), Irving, Millington (Widnes), Meek, Dixon.

WIGAN v. LEEDS

29 March 1947
Central Park, Wigan

Challenge Cup third round
Referee: T. Armitage (Huddersfield)

The most famous goal in Leeds' history came in their Challenge Cup third round tie at Wigan in 1947. It inspired Leeds to a truly epic victory and was part of an astonishing run to the cup final which saw the Loiners reach Wembley without conceding a point in their five matches en-route. The hero of the hour at Central Park was Kiwi full-back Bert Cook, who had been snapped up by the Leeds management as a member of the New Zealand Army fifteen-a-side team who had played a tour match at Headingley in 1946. He joined Leeds mid-way through the 1946/47 campaign, just a few weeks before another all-time great import, Australian Arthur Clues.

Their arrival came at the beginning of one of the worst spells of weather ever to hit the north of England, blizzard conditions wiping out professional Rugby League for a frustrating five-week period from the start of February. When the thaw eventually set in, the Rugby Football League authorities were faced with cramming in all the early rounds of the Challenge Cup before the scheduled final on 3 May. Leeds began with a two-legged tie against Barrow, winning the first game 12-0 at Headingley, and they had the home advantage again a week later as Craven Park was unfit. Leeds came through that one 6-0 and were then 5-0 victors over Hunslet at Headingley in the second round, setting up a daunting trip to Central Park.

Leeds' preparation for the game was far from ideal, as the players and management found themselves at loggerheads in a row over bonuses. The players actually held a meeting with club officials Alf Jarman and Edgar Alcock on the team coach in City Square before heading off over the Pennines to Wigan. The club were offering £12 10s, but the players wanted either £15 no tax, or £20 with tax. The players, who were on ordinary win pay of £7, eventually told the directors they would play the match and meet with them again on the Wednesday after the game. The ones who had been on duty in the earlier rounds had already pocketed £46 – £21 in ordinary money and a £25 bonus. Eventually, a bonus of £15 was agreed on, at the time the highest ever paid by the Leeds club. Club officials complained later that, after deductions and the players' bonuses, Leeds only banked between £450 and £500 from bumper Central Park gate receipts of £2,600. The thought of their record bonus must have inspired the Leeds men as they came up with one of their finest ever performances in Wigan.

The Loiners were unchanged from the previous week's win over Hunslet, with Dai Jenkins defying a heavy cold to take his place at scrum-half. The sport's dominant team at the time, Wigan were slightly below strength, but put Leeds under heavy early pressure on a grassless pitch which had been soaked by heavy rain. The standing water and clinging mud made open rugby almost impossible, but the Loiners produced a magnificent defensive display to keep the hosts at bay, with Cook and centre Gareth Price both outstanding. Price kept Leeds' line intact when he produced a superb tackle on Johnny Lawrenson, who had seemed certain to score from Ernest Ashcroft's pass, and he repeated the feat moments later to deny Cec Mountford as Wigan dominated possession on the back of a four to one success rate in the scrums. Ike Owens relieved the pressure with a break from half-way for Leeds, but Wigan snuffed out the danger and counter-attacked, only for Cook to produce a try-saving tackle on Brian Nordgren.

With both defences in mean mood, it was obviously going to take something special to break the deadlock and Cook produced it with a moment of pure magic. Even the Kiwi seemed sceptical when his skipper Owens ordered him to go for goal after Wigan had been caught off-side on half-way. But as the 33,353 crowd watched on, the full-back scraped some mud

Wigan 0   Leeds 5

A thrilling Challenge Cup campaign saw Leeds reach Wembley without conceding a point. Dai Jenkins begins another mesmeric attack with Chris Brereton in support on the inside and Ike Owens ready to receive a pinpoint pass outside him.

together to tee up the ball and then struck it magnificently straight between the posts 50 metres away. Cook's incredible goal gave Leeds new heart and seemed to demoralise Wigan, who were shocked to go in at half-time two points down. The second period brought more incredible tension as the hosts desperately tried to find a way through Leeds' magnificent defence. The action boiled over when Leeds prop Dai Prosser and his Wigan opposite number Ken Gee were sent-off for fighting, but even with the extra space, both defences remained water-tight. It looked as though Cook's goal would be enough to seal Leeds' place in the semi-final, but the game was put beyond any doubt when Price snapped up a loose pass from Joe Egan and raced over for the only try, Cook this time failing to find the target with his conversion attempt. After the 5-0 win at Wigan, Leeds were paired with neighbours Wakefield Trinity in the semi-final at Huddersfield's Fartown and yet again they kept their opponents off the scoresheet, Cook contributing a try and three goals in a 21-0 triumph.

Leeds had become the first side in the Challenge Cup's 50-year history to reach the final without conceding a point, but sadly for the Headingley men they couldn't keep that record intact in a disappointing Wembley showdown with Bradford Northern. Leeds led 2-0 at half-time thanks to a Cook penalty and the Kiwi added another after the break, but two tries and a drop goal sealed an 8-4 triumph for Bradford. Leeds finished the season in fourth place in the table to earn a return trip to Central Park in the championship semi-final, but Wigan gained full revenge for their Challenge Cup exit with a 21-11 success in a match played on 7 June. The scale of Leeds' Cup win at Central Park is illustrated by the fact Wigan won every other available honour that season, topping the table and winning the Championship, Lancashire League and Lancashire Cup.

Wigan: Ryan, Nordgren, Lawrenson, Ashcroft, Jolley, Mountford, Bradshaw, Gee, Eagan, Banks, Evans, W. Blan, J. Blan.

Leeds: Cook, Cornelius, Price, T.L. Williams, Whitehead, R. Williams, Jenkins, Prosser, Murphy, Brereton, Watson, Clues, Owens.

Leeds v. Hunslet

8 April 1955
Headingley

League match
Referee: Mr R. Gelder (Wakefield)

Some matches have everything; heroism, drama, spectacle, prodigal returns, intense local rivalry, controversy, excitement to the last – and this Easter showdown was one such fixture. Going into the Good Friday encounter, Leeds stood on the verge of the top four Championship play-offs, a feat they had achieved only once in the previous seventeen seasons. Since defeating Doncaster 26-6 in early February, none of the seven following league or cup games had been decided by a margin of more than six points as the tension and expectation level rose among the Loiners fans. From the end of November, when Batley were vanquished at Mount Pleasant through to a surprise defeat at York in mid-March, Leeds had lost only once in the regular season when they were resoundingly beaten 13-2 by Hunslet at Parkside. Their disappointment that day was heightened when new signing Joe Anderson from Castleford suffered a dislocated shoulder in only his second appearance in the blue and amber. Over 22,500 fans turned up to Headingley for the return match, which

had an unusual 5.30 p.m. kick-off, and most had come to see one man, Arthur Clues on his return to the ground where he had become a cult figure over nine glorious years. The dynamic, fearless Australian, who had played in three Tests Down Under prior to his shock capture by Leeds, won few medals but a legion of fervent admirers for his uncompromising, multi-skilled style of play. His distaste for authority was almost as legendary as his on-field prowess and rumours had abounded from the start of the 1954/55 campaign that the then thirty-year-old was on the verge of being surplus to requirements. Nevertheless, it came as a shock and feverish point of debate throughout the city when he was allowed to join Hunslet in early October 1954. There he linked up with terrier-like stand-off Dicky Williams who had made a similar move across the river nine months earlier to equal howls of protest from the Leeds aficionados.

Hunslet were coming off a narrow Challenge Cup semi-final defeat to Barrow and named a full strength side while Leeds had Australian

Arthur Clues as the Leeds fans remembered him on his arrival at Headingley in 1947. He took club officials by surprise when his plane touched down five days earlier than expected despite stopping off at Darwin, Singapore, Calcutta, Palestine and Malta en route to London.

Leeds 22   Hunslet 12

centre Keith McLellan back after being out for a month with a throat injury although youngster Jeff Stevenson was called up to replace World Cup star Gordon Brown. Encounters with so many tasty side issues rarely live up to their billing but this one was an exception, the heightened anticipation more than met in a match that rightly carried the label 'classic'.

Leeds opened in cavalier fashion, Lewis Jones nearly getting winger Dennis Scholes away on the left before a superb transfer of the ball across the three-quarters saw Drew Turnbull crash over in the opposite corner with barely two minutes on the clock. With the heavyweight Hunslet pack back-pedalling, Stevenson began a virtuoso performance that dominated the proceedings. His searing break up the middle split the visiting line and with the cover closing in, a majestic one handed pass from head height freed Jones in acres of space who cantered round to the posts to double the lead. Stevenson was then involved in the most contentious incident of the night in the 25th minute when he tangled with Hunslet winger Snowden on the far side. Touch judge Mr W. Harrison immediately raised his flag and came on to the field of action, his intervention seeing Snowden summarily dismissed from the play although few could see the circumstances that warranted it. With penalties swapped in the run up to the break, Leeds held a comfortable 12-2 lead and looked set for a handsome win.

The opening exchanges at the start of the second half changed all that with Clues and tearaway young back-rower Geoff Gunney ripping into the home ranks belying their numerical disadvantage. Clues effortlessly sidestepped youngster Bill Hanson, who some had said on his arrival from Oldham was earmarked as his replacement, and with Talbot's conversion the visitors were in the ascendancy. Magnificent scrambling defence denied Dicky Williams, Clues again, Gunney when seemingly a certain scorer, Shaw and Smith, McLellan bravely playing on with a broken nose in a desperate rearguard action. In the 52nd minute, Talbot hit a post with a penalty attempt from 20 yards out and with it Hunslet's chance was gone. Stevenson's pace off the mark again caught them cold and in the words of esteemed *Yorkshire Post* reporter Alfred Drewery, 'taking the ball in his own half, went left, then right, beating men all the time; turned round in his tracks to beat more and, finally, when he seemed cornered, flicked a cheeky reverse pass to McLellan, who found Jones waiting on the right touchline for the scoring pass.' That dazzling try was the turning point for no matter how tirelessly Clues foraged and Gunney pounded the home ranks, a mercurial dart from Stevenson carried Leeds out of trouble. Late on, his three mesmeric sidesteps again created havoc allowing prop Tony Skelton in support to crash over. Gunney's try in the final minute was no less than he deserved as honour was satisfied all round.

Clues was given a rapturous ovation and left the Leeds board in no doubt that his talents were not yet on the wane. Dicky Williams, who had captained the Lions tourists the year before after being released by the Loiners, showed he still retained his deft touches while Stevenson, a month short of his twenty-third birthday, announced his arrival at the top table, his distinguished international career beginning later that year. Victory brought the Loiners the Yorkshire League title for the ninth time, but they still needed three points from their remaining three matches to clinch a play-off berth. Defeat by a point the following day at Featherstone was followed by a 13-all draw at Wheldon Road on the Monday, with Turnbull's five tries accounting for Wakefield at Headingley in final match of the season to claim third spot in the standings. A tight first half at the Watersheddings gave hope of an appearance in the Championship final, but the Holy Grail was to be denied for another year when injuries to Stevenson and Jones saw Oldham run out easy 25-6 winners.

Leeds: Dunn, Turnbull, McLellan, Jones, Broughton, Stevenson, Pratt, Skelton, Wood, Anderson, Poole, Hanson, Last.

Hunslet: Talbot, Snowden, Evans, Harrison, L. Williams, R. Williams, Gabbitas, Smith, Shaw, Burnell, Gunney, Clues, James.

Leeds v. Australia

13 October 1956
Headingley

Kangaroo tour match
Referee: R. Gelder (Wakefield)

The lure of Headingley has enticed many an Australian to sign for Leeds, often without prior confirmation of terms. Its unique dual Test arena steeped in epic battle for the Ashes in both rugby and cricket is a huge draw for those born in the land of the green and gold. Some of Australia's most famous names have exhibited their sublime skills on the Leeds turf, while others eager to impress in one of the spiritual homes of the thirteen-a-side code have arrived as unknowns and returned home to wear representative jerseys with distinction. Virtually every one of the Aussies to have played for Leeds have become ambassadors for the club, singing its praises to the next generation with some such as Dinny Campbell, Arthur Clues and Ted Verrenkamp actively recruiting to keep the strong association going. The majority of the Kangaroo touring teams have spent extensive time in and around the city and seventeen of them have met the side representing their hosts, Leeds only missing out on an available match in 1973. The Loiners have only prevailed on three occasions: in 1929 by the odd point in 15; thanks to the efforts of compatriots Vic Hey and two try Eric Harris in 1937 and latterly in 1956 when returning favourite and skipper Ken Kearney was on the receiving end. His charges found their feet with an easy win at Liverpool City, before running out at Headingley in front of nearly 25,000 fervent fans. There was a certain irony about the turn out, it being the highest on tour beating attendances for the Second and Third Tests staged at Bradford and Swinton in preference to Leeds. There was disappointment among the home following when it was announced that Lewis Jones was an absentee but centre Don Gullick was added to the ranks on loan from Leigh to play the first of fifteen appearances in blue and amber.

With an entire first-choice three-quarter line missing, the Loiners were forced to reshuffle with Pat Quinn moved to centre and Derek Wilkinson shifted out to the wing. Captain Keith McLellan relished the chance to be pitted against the men from his homeland while 'Kearney's Kangaroos' contained six men who were to line up in the opening Test at Wigan a month later although the legendary Clive Churchill – whose Test career was to come to end at Central Park – was not among them. The tourists opened in sensational fashion, dominating the early exchanges through their powerful pack and inventive and vastly experienced halves Ian Johnston of Parramatta and the irrepressible Keith Holman. Norm Provan would have secured the opening points but for a forward pass from Queensland centre Alex Watson before the point of attack switched to the left, winger Ian Moir powering over for an unconverted try near the corner flag and being hauled down just short soon after. Churchill's replacement, Newtown's Gordon Clifford, missed a penalty and only a relieving run from Gullick in the 12th minute cleared the home lines.

The respite was temporary, prop Roy Bull putting the Kangaroos back on the charge but a remarkable counter attack changed the balance of power. Leeds were desperately defending their own line and were awarded a scrum in the shadow of the posts. Snap interplay between young scrum-half Billy Pratt and the vastly experienced Harry Street set the rangy loose-forward on an unstoppable run to halfway. A quick play the ball and Jeff Stevenson, filling the number six shirt, scampered clear with a mazy run. Just as the Aussies thought they had steered him up a blind alley, a pinpoint cross-kick saw McLellan in acres of space field the ball and joyously plunge over wide out, Jimmy Dunn missing the extras. Kearney put his charges back on the attack with Holman busy and back-row Tom Tyquin a handful but Gullick was again the catalyst for escapology, Dunn's touchfinder putting pressure on the visiting line. Big

Leeds 18   Australia 13

The 1956 Kangaroos. From left to right, back row: C.B. Churchill, K.V. Holman, C.W. Connell, I.J. Johnston, D.P. Adams, I.J. Moir. Third row: E.A. Hammerton, R.B. Banks, K.V. O'Brien, R.H. Poole, B.M. Purcell, L.R. Payne, G.L. Clifford. Second row: W.L. Marsh, I.R.P. Doyle, B.J. Orrock, T.J. Tyquin, B. Davies, D.J. McGovern, A. Watson, D.A. Furner. Front row: E.R. Bull, B.D. Provan, C. Fahy (manager), K.H. Keraney, C. Connell (manager), K.J. O'Shea, D.J. Flannery.

Joe Anderson held up the ball to perfection allowing Don Robinson to crash through would be tackles on a barnstorming run to the posts, Dunn's conversion making it 8-3 at the break.

In a reversal of the opening exchanges, it was Leeds who dominated the start of the second half, the pack creating quality possession for centres Quinn and McLellan to flex their muscles. Against them, Watson was having a magnificent match and it was his arcing run to the wing that allowed Moir to cut inside to collect his second try, the conversion levelling matters. Minutes later and Holman was dancing down the middle to score, Clifford's easy goal puting the visitors 13-8 up and seemingly in control for their customary win. Only some heroic scrambling defence kept them out as Leeds gradually fought their way back to set up a dramatic last quarter.

Kearney was withdrawn after needing stitches in a nasty facial wound and with the Loiners guaranteed a majority of possession as a result, they took charge. With less than ten minutes left, Billy Pratt found the smallest of gaps on the blind side to scamper over, Dunn bringing parity with his successful conversion. Stevenson – who was to play a key role in all three Ashes Tests – danced tirelessly in attack, prompting Bull's frustrations to get the better of him and as the crowd roared their heroes home, Street and Robinson conjured one last move which put Bernard Prior in the clear, the hooker romping across the whitewash to the obvious delight of virtually all in the ground. Dunn's conversion was academic but no less significant for that as Leeds held on for a famous win. The confidence gained saw them embark on a then club record-breaking 18-match winning run from the end of November to mid-March which eventually culminated in a win over Barrow at Wembley. For the Aussies, the Ashes series was lost 2-1, injuries to key men scuppering their chances, their final record in Britain seeing them win 10 and lose 9 of their matches. Lewis Jones was to smash the points-in-a-season record with 496 but as well as not playing in this match, he also missed out on the Tests.

Leeds: Dunn, Wilkinson, McLellan, Quinn, Gullick, Stevenson, Pratt, Anderson, Prior, Hopper, Poole, Robinson, Street.

Australia: Clifford, Adams, Watson, O'Brien, Moir, Johnston, Holman, Orrock, Kearney, Bull, Tyquin, Provan, Doyle.

HALIFAX v. LEEDS

9 March 1957
Thrum Hall, Halifax

Challenge Cup third round
Referee: Mr C.F. Appleton (Warrington)

Cup fever is always likely to break out at Headingley and 1957 was no exception. Excitement was magnified by the first round draw, which saw Wigan come to Leeds in front of a packed crowd with thousands locked outside. The Riversiders were unbeaten in twelve games and twice ahead by a point following two sensational tries from Billy Boston, but a superb drop goal by Lewis Jones and tries to Del Hodgkinson and skipper Keith McLellan ensured a dramatic 13-11 success. Hopes were higher when it was discovered that Warrington had been drawn, again at headquarters, in the second round. Heavy snow nearly saw off the contest but, once the pitch had been cleared and the lines continually swept during play, an impressive six-try performance put paid to the men from Wilderspool.

If fortune had been with Leeds in the opening rounds, a quarter-final trip to Thrum Hall would have been one of their least favoured options. The previous season Halifax had knocked them out at the same stage and the Loiners' record there in cup football was poor. The hosts were installed as favourites despite Leeds coming into the game on the back of a fifteen-match winning run, with a capacity crowd of 27,500 guaranteed. In the week leading up to the game black market ticket values set new records. Conditions at the tight, sloping venue were muddy but Halifax scrum-half Stan Keilty's wish for a cloudburst at three o'clock, 'to slow them down a bit' failed to materialise.

The Headingley management had decided against sending the team away for intensified preparation for fear that the players' nerves would be heightened but in the early stages of the fiercest of encounters that decision looked to have backfired. Five penalties were awarded with four players warned by referee Mr Appleton, Garfield Owen kicking the opening points for Halifax from wide out after Leeds were penalised at the play-the-ball. The sense of the occasion was clearly evident when Lewis Jones, in a season in which he was to break most of the individual scoring records, missed two eminently kickable opportunities in reply. Heartened by those reprieves, the home pack through Thorley and Ackerley took charge, Keilty's kick to the corner forcing Jones to concede a scrum as he scrambled the ball away into touch. Keilty's quick switch found loose-forward Ken Traill powering up on the inside and he took three Leeds men over the line with him for the opening score, Owen just missing with the conversion attempt. Eight minutes later and it seemed the game was up, Traill again the destroyer as his wonderful sidestep took him past Don Robinson, Bernard Poole and Pat Quinn for a mesmerising score to which Owen this time added the extras.

Ten points down in twenty minutes and Leeds' cup dreams were seemingly in tatters – although no one had told McLellan. Constantly pleading and urging his men on in midfield and invariably taking the ball to give his forwards a breather, his galvanising example began to pay off. Hooker Bernard Prior won three crucial scrums in succession and Jones slotted over a penalty before Poole engineered a gap for stand-off Jack Lendill and he left Traill and Owen floundering for a terrific score. Jones' goal made it 10-7 at the break and, when Keilty was penalised at the start of the second half, his third successful kick narrowed the gap to a point. Leeds wingers Hodgkinson and George Broughton were just denied by fine, despairing tackles from Owen but a magnificent disguised pass by Traill put centre Harper Daniels clear, his fifty yard burst ending as he was just bundled into the corner flag. The Halifax pack camped in the visiting quarter but Leeds produced their most spirited form in adversity with Harry Street leading the heroic resistance. In the 65th minute, it was his break that set

---

Halifax 10   Leeds 16

Joyous scenes greeted the side as they returned triumphant after beating Barrow in the final at Wembley and inched their way to the Town Hall to be congratulated by the Lord Mayor of Leeds Alderman T.A. Jessop.

Hodgkinson racing into the clear only for another play-the-ball infringement to give Jones the chance to put Leeds ahead for the first time. A few paces in from touch on the 25 yard line and with so much hanging on the outcome, the pressure on the kicker must have been intolerable but the aim was true and the outcome never in doubt. In the final minutes there was drama at both ends; Pearce just denied by three Leeds tacklers, Hodgkinson falling to Owen with the line beckoning and in the last seconds Johnny Freeman thought he had scored only to plunge for the Leeds line a yard short. Street made a half break, Hodgkinson sprinted clear down the wing and fittingly his inside pass found McLellan cantering half the length of the field to the posts, Jones' conversion bringing the curtain down on a remarkable, gutsy performance.

The closeness of the sides was verified by the statistics, Halifax taking the scrums 17-16 and the 32 penalties being shared. Long serving members of the Leeds pack Poole and Ernie Hopper both declared that the win was one of the finest moments of their career but Cumbria stood in the way of ultimate glory. Two Broughton tries and a snap Jeff Stevenson drop goal two minutes from time accounted for obdurate Whitehaven at Odsal and although the final at Wembley never rose to the heights expected, a nerve-wracking 9-7 win over Barrow – with Stevenson taking the Lance Todd Trophy – was enough to bring the Cup back to Headingley.

Halifax: Owen, Asquith, Daniels, Dean, Freeman, Broadhurst, Keilty, Thorley, Ackerley, Wilkinson, Pearce, Clift, Traill.

Leeds: Quinn, Hodgkinson, McLellan, Jones, Broughton, Lendill, Stevenson, Anderson, Prior, Hopper, Poole, Robinson, Street.

Leeds v. Wakefield Trinity

18 October 1958
Odsal, Bradford

Yorkshire Cup final
Referee: C.F. Appleton (Warrington)

Hooker Barry Simms played 142 times for Leeds, but is best remembered his first appearance in a knockout tie when he helped the Loiners end a long and embarrassing trophy drought. Simms, then aged just nineteen, deputised for the injured Bernard Prior in the 1958 Yorkshire Cup final and played a starring role as Leeds lifted the famous prize for the first time in twenty-one years. Leeds had opened their Yorkshire Cup campaign in a blaze of glory with a 64-17 home thrashing of Huddersfield, Del Hodgkinson scoring six tries and Lewis Jones chipping in with a hat-trick and seven goals, just hours after a fire had caused severe damage to the Headingley pavilion. Keith McLellan's 69th and final try for Leeds secured a 17-15 win over visitors Keighley in the second round and they then hung on for a tense 13-10 triumph over York at Clarence Street in the semi-final.

Leeds had not won the Yorkshire Cup since beating Huddersfield in the 1937 decider and the omens two decades later were not good. The Loiners struggled badly in the month between the semi-final and their Odsal meeting with Wakefield, crashing 47-17 at home to Warrington just a week before the final. That game saw Prior suffer a rib injury and Simms was called in from the Alliance side for only his sixth senior appearance and his first in any cup tie. Worried Simms would lose out to Wakefield's John Shaw in the battle for scrum possession, the Leeds management went for mobility in the pack, switching Colin Tomlinson from prop to second-row, with Alec Dick moving back to displace Trevor Whitehead at loose-forward. In the backs, Pat Quinn moved to full-back and Jack Lendill was recalled at centre, with Gordon Brown continuing at stand-off. Captain and coach Ken Traill was passed fit for Wakefield and his dilemma over whether to choose Eric Lockwood or Frank Mortimer at full-back was resolved when the former slipped at work the day before the game and aggravated an old ankle injury.

Wakefield went into the game as favourites and were making their sixth post-war appearance in the final. Their four wins since the end of hostilities included a replay victory over the Loiners in 1947, the last time Leeds had reached the final. As it turned out, Leeds' fears over the inexperienced Simms' ball-winning abilities proved unfounded. Though Leeds lost the scrums 15-13 overall, Simms was on top when it really mattered. Three times in the first half he snatched possession at a scrum near the Trinity line and each time Leeds scored. Simms capped a memorable afternoon with a try himself just before the break and though Wakefield staged a storming comeback in the second half, the cup was already in the Headingley bag. Leeds were on top from the start with new skipper Jeff Stevenson, Simms and Don Robinson directing play in an all-out assault on the Trinity line, which ended when Jones was off-target with an early shot at goal. Traill, back at the ground where he had starred for Bradford Northern, led a counter-attack which saw Neil Fox, Sam Evans and Keith Holliday all go close before Fox broke the deadlock with a penalty goal on 16 minutes.

Their lead lasted just two minutes. Mortimer's superb tackle denied Garry Hemingway after a thrilling run, but Simms heeled the scrum and a planned move by Brown and Stevenson saw the scrum-half shoot over for Jones to add the goal. Again Mortimer denied Hemingway, but again the move led to a scrum which brought a Leeds try, this time Quinn bursting over from Brown's pass, Jones adding the extras. Trinity replied on the half hour when Fox sent Don Metcalfe over for an unconverted try, but that was a momentary setback for Leeds who added two more touchdowns before the interval. First Dick, Stevenson and

Leeds 24   Wakefield Trinity 20

LEEDS v. WAKEFIELD TRINITY

Jeff Stevenson's men finally won back the County Cup after 21 years with the skipper and Lance Todd trophy winner from the year before again inspirational when it really mattered.

Brown linked up after another scrum heel by Simms to send Jones over, though the Welshman could not convert, and then Simms completed his fairytale, starting and finishing the move for the Loiners' fourth try. The teenager pounced on a loose ball and broke clear from near his own line before sending Fred Ward away. Fox got across to make the tackle, but couldn't prevent Ward getting the ball back to Simms who nipped over for a wonderful score, converted by Jones. Fox landed a goal, after Stevenson had been penalised for illegally feeding a scrum in front of his own posts, but at 18-7 down at the break there was no way back for Trinity. Spring-heeled winger Hemingway struck twice early in the second period to make the game absolutely safe for Leeds. He was shoved into touch near the try-line after great build-up play by Brown and Lendill, but made no mistake soon afterwards when he raced over after intercepting Fox's pass, Jones failing to convert. Hemingway finished off a crisp passing move for the Loiners' sixth try to open up a 24-7 lead and the celebrations were already underway on the Odsal terraces.

Wakefield refused to throw in the towel and tries by Metcalfe and Ken Rollin, with Mortimer adding a goal, reduced Leeds' advantage to nine points with nine minutes to go. The Loiners held out comfortably through the final stages and Metcalfe's hat-trick try, converted by Mortimer with the last kick of the game, was mere consolation. The historic Yorkshire Cup win, in what was up to then the highest-scoring final in the competition's history, was the one highlight of a disappointing season for Leeds. Their mediocrity was illustrated by a league record of 19 wins and 19 defeats, scoring 608 points and conceding 653, for a 14th place finish in the table.

Leeds: Quinn, Hemingway, J. Lendill, Jones, Hodgkinson, Brown, Stevenson, Skelton, Simms, Tomlinson, Robinson, Ward, Dick.

Wakefield Trinity: Mortimer, F. Smith, Metcalfe, N. Fox, S. Smith, Holliday, Rollin, Adams, Shaw, Evans, Kelly, Chamberlain, Traill.

Leeds v. Warrington

20 May 1961
Odsal, Bradford

Championship final
Referee: R. Gelder (Wilmslow)

Some of the most illustrious names to grace the famous colours of the Leeds club had tried and failed to bring the trophy dubbed the 'Holy Grail' back to Headingley. On five occasions in the sixty-six years since their entry as founder members of the Northern Union, the Loiners had reached the decider to determine the ultimate Champions only for Huddersfield three times – including a heart-wrenching replay in 1929/30 – Swinton and Hunslet to take the ultimate spoils. A whole generation had passed since the all-Leeds battle of 1938 which had been the Loiners' last attempt, but twenty-three years later the omens were positive for one of the most famous names in the game to break its inconceivable drought.

Leeds had been in sensational form all season, their settled squad playing a wonderful brand of flowing, vastly entertaining rugby to register 30 victories from their 36 league fixtures, their best ever return, which saw them end the regular season campaign at the top of the table for the first time in the club's history and with the best defensive record. There had been one major signing, international loose-forward Brian Shaw moving to the north of the city from Hunslet just before the Challenge Cup deadline for a reported world record fee of £13,250, although Bernard Prior and Norman Burton went to Parkside in exchange as part of the deal. Wigan, after a replay, saw to it that the dream of Wembley was extinguished in the opening round of the Challenge Cup but that only served to strengthen the resolve of the Leeds squad to write their names in legend.

In the Championship semi-final at Headingley, a star-studded St Helens outfit – who were to win at the Twin Towers a week later – proved to be typically unyielding in the first meeting between the sides that season. Many neutrals felt that Leeds had come through an easier run of fixtures and that their red rose rivals, who had by far the best attack in the competition, would find them out especially as boom young centre Fred Pickup – who was destined to star for Parramatta in later years – was ruled out with injury, novice Vince Hattee taking his place. More than 19,000 frenzied fans braved the elements to see the battle royal, with a spiteful late spring wind whipping round the ground and dictating the early tactics.

Using it to his advantage, Leeds skipper Lewis Jones kicked a long range penalty to open the scoring before Dennis Goodwin split the Saints cover to send smiling South African winger Wilf Rosenberg diving spectacularly in at the corner for his 43rd try of the season, thereby setting a new post-war club record of touchdowns. Magnificent scrambling defence, particularly when Jones denied McGinn on one flank and notably by Eddie Ratcliffe to continually scupper dangerman Van Vollenhoven on the other, restricted Saints to a penalty in reply, before another superb Jones touchfinder set the position for Hattee to claim the try spoils. A second penalty by Rhodes to make it 8-4 immediately raised the stakes at the start of the second half, the visitors dominating territorially with the wind at their backs but no quarter being given as Jack Fairbank and Barry Simms in particular worked overtime to thwart the likes of the rampaging Karalius and Vines.

The frantic denouement fifteen minutes from time conjured one of the most treasured tries witnessed on Headingley's famous, lush turf. Simms, Evans and Hallas led the break out giving Rosenberg a tilt from forty yards out. Sullivan, Watson and Rhodes were all beaten by his sheer pace on a thrilling straight dash for the corner and the way to Odsal finally cleared.

Leeds 25   Warrington 10

The Leeds squad which made history by capturing the 'Holy Grail' after a wait of sixty-six long years. From left to right, back row: T. Whitehead, J. Fairbank, D. Robinson, D. Goodwin, B. Shaw, K.W. Thornett, B. Simms. Front row: V.N. Hattee, W. Rosenberg, D. Hallas, B.L. Jones, F. Pickup, E. Ratcliffe, C. Evans.

Keeping St Helens try-less in such a fiercely fought contest was seen as auguring well for the ultimate clash with Cec Mountford's Warrington, who had ended the regular season as runners up in the standings on points difference ahead of Swinton.

When Leeds had won at Wembley for the first time in 1936, it was the men from Wilderspool who provided the opposition but sentiment counted for nothing against a fearsome Wire side which included internationals Eric Fraser, Jim Challinor and Laurie Gilfedder alongside all-time try scoring legend, Australian wizard Brian Bevan. Manager Joe Warham and coach, former international prop and Headingley stalwart Dai Prosser, named an unchanged line up from the semi-final for the Loiners. The significant difference in the opening exchanges seemed to be the desire of the younger Leeds legions as they tore into their opposing numbers in a frenzied start, the 52,177 Whitsuntide crowd roaring their approval in appreciation of the fast and furious action in the watery sunshine. In among the opening bombardment as the respective packs tested each out, Leeds supremo Jones directed and marshalled with characteristic authority, sending nerveless centre Hattee on a couple of early rampaging charges before scurrying back to deny Gilfedder.

Leeds: Thornett, Rosenberg, Hallas, Hattee, Ratcliffe, Jones, Evans, Robinson, Simms, Whitehead, Fairbank, Goodwin, Shaw.
Warrington: Fraser, Bevan, Challinor, Pickavance, O'Grady, Greenhough, Edwards, Brindle, Harper, Arkwright, Gilfedder, Major, Naughton.

LEEDS v. WARRINGTON

With their forwards magnificently led by second-rowers Fairbank and Goodwin, Leeds gradually gained supremacy thanks to the unerring ferocity of their defence which constantly harried their opposing numbers and the radar-like accuracy of Jones' hefty boot which continually turned Warrington round, although his first shot at goal following a foul by Jackie Edwards slipped wide of the posts. Gaps began to be created, Don Robinson just failing to take Simms' scoring pass, but the opening points were not long in coming, Fairbank proving unstoppable as he crashed over at the side of the sticks courtesy of Goodwin's disguised pass, Jones converting to make it 5-0 after a quarter of an hour. Hooker Simms was having the match of his life, crucially out striking his opposite number Harper three to one in the scrums to ensure endless quality possession for the Leeds halves to work their oracle. Rosenberg and Jones were denied in cover with Warrington restricted to two failed penalty attempts, the first from Fraser glancing off a post, before the Yorkshiremen cut loose in thrilling style. Full-back Ken Thornett was the instigator with a brilliant clearing run, Hattee, Derek Hallas and Jones carried the momentum to near the posts and livewire scrum-half Colin Evans darted over from acting-half-back to double the lead as half-time approached.

The first score after the interval was always likely to be the game breaker and Leeds began in irresistible fashion, perhaps sensing their destiny, pulling the Warrington defence from left to right and back again as they searched for a chink in the wilting line. The interplay between backs and forwards was mesmerising: Hattee, Jones, Simms and Trevor Whitehead were all frantically denied in increasingly despairing cover, but the wave was building behind the Wire dam. When it broke the damage was critical, centre Hallas – in perhaps his finest hour – romping over for a brace of touchdowns in quick succession thanks to wonderful offloads from first Whitehead as he fell in the tackle and then Thornett after another Jones break to make it 18-0.

With the joyous blue and amber hordes on the terraces beginning to celebrate long awaited history in the making, Challinor heroically staged a last, desperate fightback interspersing a Jones penalty with two tries, the first a clever interception, both converted by Gilfedder to make it 20-10 – but they were nothing more than consolation. Any wavering doubts among the Leeds fans were assuaged by their exceptional skipper who would surely have taken the man of the match award – the Harry Sunderland Trophy not being inaugurated until four years later. With the Warrington defence back-pedalling, Jones jinked

Derek Hallas careers over for the first of his two quick-fire tries.

No stopping scrum half Colin Evans as he drives to the posts to make it 10-0 just before half-time with fellow Welshman, skipper Lewis Jones, looking on.

one way and then stepped the other to touchdown at the side of the posts in one of the most photographed images in the history of the club. Many a grown man missed his chipped conversion to make it 25-10 as they dried their eyes, overcome by the emotion and significance of it. It was only fitting that the balding maestro should gleefully hold aloft the missing jewel in the crown. The win was immediately dedicated to former chairman Rex Proctor who had tragically died in a road accident in South Wales a few weeks before and was cruelly denied the chance to see the fruits of his labour.

LEEDS v. HALIFAX

30 March 1964   Championship
Headingley   Referee: Mr C.F. Appleton (Warrington)

Rugby League is the ultimate team sport, but occasionally an individual comes along who dominates his generation. Lewis Jones was one, signed in a blaze of glory in November 1952 for the then princely sum of £6,000 and he immediately earned the tag 'golden boy'. Few of the Leeds fans who followed his development into a record-breaking points scorer for both club and country over the next twelve seasons could claim that he was anything less. Alfred Drewery, the respected Rugby League writer for the *Yorkshire Post* when reporting on this, his last of 385 appearances in the blue and amber, called him the 'Great Exasperator', his genius being such that when in full bloom he could win a match single-handedly, while anything which appeared to be slightly less than his best was perceived as diffidence. Leeds fans idolised him and there is little doubt that his name on the teamsheet was the code's major draw at the time, home or away. His greatest season was 1957, which saw him pick up a Wembley winner's medal and create a host of scoring milestones, many of which still stand. What gave him tremendous satisfaction was that his final world best tally of 496 points for club and country from a total of 51 matches bettered the mark set by one of his own heroes, another legendary Welshman Jim Sullivan. Statistics, though, only tell part of the story. In that season alone his sublime skill and versatility was such that he played in ten different positions in successive games. His greatest legacy for the adoring Headingley faithful was undoubtedly his captain's performance as the Championship was finally collected at Odsal in 1961. Now aged thirty-three, he had decided to emigrate to Australia to take up the offer of player/coach at Wentworthville in the Sydney second division.

This Easter Monday fixture was Leeds' third in four days of a mediocre season although he did not play in the defeat at Hunslet on the Friday or in the win over Batley the following day. Over 17,000 fans had seen him make his debut but pitifully just under 8,000 witnessed the farewell, Jones taking his place at stand-off in an inexperienced side ravaged by injuries, with young second-rower Ernest Towler making his debut after signing from Yorkshire Copper Works. Before the game there were presentations on the pitch, Noel Stockdale the football chairman handing over a silver cigarette box on behalf of the directors and Tom Steel, president of the Leeds Supporters' Club, an inscribed coffee set. Halifax won the toss and took advantage of a strong wind, Jones kicking off a match at Headingley for the final time. His first long punt downfield in general play failed to find touch but from then on there was a sense that the young Leeds side were playing as though something significant was at stake.

At the heart of the best rugby was the man around whom all the attention was based. The first time he had the ball in hand he instigated a sparkling attack, breaking clear in midfield with a characteristic step before sending out a wonderful long pass which cut out centre Drew Broatch and gave winger Alan Smith a long run. With pressure on their line Halifax full-back James attempted a long clearing kick only to send the ball directly to Leeds winger Geoff Wrigglesworth. Quickly sizing up the options he elected for a long punt to the corner just beating James and despairing covering loose-forward Renilson to the ball on a thrilling chase for an excellent try. By then Jones had surrendered the goalkicking to up and coming local youngster Robin Dewhirst and he did the master proud with an angled conversion into the elements.

Leeds 16   Halifax 7

Welsh wizard Lewis Jones' proudest moment of a twelve-year career which thrilled and enthralled Leeds fans as he raises the Championship Trophy at Odsal with Don Robinson alongside him – the first men in the club's history to hold Challenge Cup and Championship winners' medals.

The visitors hit back, the play punctuated by frequent warnings to hookers Chamberlain and Shaw who seemed determined to carry on their own private battle and bottle up the play in midfield at the same time. Halifax halves Marchant and Kellett began giving the ball some width, Jackson raiding down the right wing before effortless passing across the three-quarters freed Hudson on the left for a fine touchdown. Niggling tactics continued to dominate, with only the occasional dash from Jones lightening the proceedings, James and Dewhirst swapping penalties as a result to leave it tied at 7-7 at the break. The second half started in sensational fashion, Jones with the wind at his back arrowing a prodigious kick downfield and forcing a scrum on the Halifax 25-yard line.

When it erupted, Mr Appleson had little hesitation in dismissing both number nines and the match improved immeasurably as a spectacle as a result. Leeds seemed determined to make sure that their talisman went out a winner and with more space to exploit, Jones began dazzling the faithful with his dashing runs and creative darts. South African loose-forward Louis Neumann stayed in close support, his powerful runs driving the visitors back while Broatch in the centre looked an increasingly dangerous threat. Dewhirst kicked a magnificent penalty from the halfway line to put the Loiners ahead and stand in hooker Les Chamberlain began to dominate possession. Former Batley forward Peter McVeigh tore into the Halifax ranks and as Fogerty desperately tried to raise the siege, Alan Smith stepped inside to intercept and power to the corner for a fine, opportunist score.

Dewhirst's conversion from the touchline on the opposite side to his first brought widespread acclaim and an appreciable nod from Jones. Another tiptoeing break up the middle nearly brought the maestro a touchdown but the only other score was another penalty from Dewhirst, as he finished the game with five out of five successes. On the final whistle, the crowd stayed on to bid fond farewell to their departing star, although ironically for a man who shattered virtually every points scoring record for the club he had failed to register for only the 29th time in the Leeds colours. The tremendous memories he left were incalculable and his legacy outstanding; as he departed his favourite field for the last time it was as Loiners' fifth highest appearance maker, fourth best try-scorer and leading goal marksman and points gatherer. It was largely because of his outstanding talents that Wentworthville went on to become virtually unbeatable in their Metropolitan League.

Leeds: Dewhirst, Smith, Broatch, Gemmell, Wrigglesworth, Jones, Shoebottom, Thomas, Lockwood, Chamberlain, Towler, McVeigh, Neumann.

Halifax: James, Jackson, Burnett, Jones, Hudson, Kellett, Marchant, Scroby, Shaw, Duffy, Dixon, Fogerty, Renilson.

LEEDS v. WAKEFIELD TRINITY

11 May 1968
Wembley

Challenge Cup final
Referee: Mr J.P. Hebblethwaite (York)

There's an old saying that no one ever remembers Cup final losers. That wasn't the case with the 1968 Challenge Cup decider, which because of one incident has become probably the most famous game of Rugby League ever played in Great Britain. Even those with no interest in Rugby League can name Wakefield Trinity as that year's vanquished side, but they would be hard pressed to recall that it was Leeds who actually lifted the trophy. What became known as the Watersplash final would have been largely forgotten by everyone outside the competing cities but for the unfortunate Don Fox. One of Wakefield's greats, and the day's outstanding player, Fox earned himself an unwanted place in British sporting history when he missed a last second conversion attempt, from right in front of the posts, which would have given Trinity a 12-11 victory.

The final between runaway league leaders Leeds and the side who finished in second place, Wakefield, should have been a classic, but was reduced to farce by torrential rain which turned the normally immaculate Wembley playing surface into a lake. Open football was impossible as players slithered, slid, splashed and swam around a field more than ankle deep in water. The pitch had already been saturated when players from both teams took part in the traditional walkabout 24 hours before kick-off. More spectacular downpours in the hour before the first whistle and at half-time reduced the match to a lottery, but with 87,100 fans in the ground, most of them down from the north of England for the day, it was decided the show must go on. Leeds seemed to have the Cup in their grasp when Bev Risman landed a long-range penalty goal to give the Loiners an 11-7 lead with just two minutes left. But the Leeds defence couldn't control the re-start on the waterlogged surface and Ken Hirst dribbled through to touch down between the posts, putting Wakefield just a point behind with the kick to come.

Most of Leeds' players and their fans in the big crowd couldn't bear to look as Fox, who had taken over kicking duties in the absence of injured brother Neil, lined up what would in normal circumstances have been the simplest of conversion attempts. As BBC commentator Eddie Waring warned the millions of armchair viewers: 'It's not a hard shot, but it's always a hard shot when the match depends on it.' Those turned out to be prophetic words. As he stepped up to take the kick, Fox stumbled slightly and sent his effort agonisingly wide, the final whistle sounding as the touch judges indicated the miss.

As the Leeds team began their unexpected celebrations the unfortunate Fox slumped to his knees in anguish and the sympathetic Waring summed up his despair with two words: 'Poor lad'. That kick earned Fox, pictured later shedding tears of anguish, everlasting national fame and more than 30 years later it remains Rugby League's abiding image. In 2001, Fox's miss was the code's only representative in a national poll to select history's 100 most memorable sporting moments. It was also the only kick featured on the BBC's compilation video of Rugby League's 100 classic tries. The 1968 great escape was Leeds' first Challenge Cup final win for 11 years and capped a run which had seen them overcome Liverpool City, Bramley and Oldham before a golden semi-final victory over Wigan at Swinton's Station Road. Leeds had lost to the Cherry and Whites in their five previous Challenge Cup meetings, but put the record straight in scintillating style, winger John Atkinson setting them on their way to a 25-4 triumph with a majestic touchdown rated as one of the finest of his 340 in blue and amber. Atkinson was also in the thick of the action – or perhaps that should be the deep end – in the

Leeds 11   Wakefield Trinity 10

Loiners skipper Mick Clark brings the Cup home after an eleven year wait – ironically the sun shone.

final, his slip allowing Wakefield to take the lead before he was controversially awarded a penalty try to swing the game Leeds' way.

Two Risman penalty goals, against one by Fox, gave the Loiners an early advantage, but Wakefield sailed into a 7-4 interval lead when Atkinson lost his footing attempting to reach Fox's deep kick and Hirst took advantage to hack over for the try, converted by Fox. Another downpour at half-time made conditions even worse and there looked to be no way back for Leeds until another dramatic twist 10 minutes from time. Atkinson kicked ahead and collided with Wakefield centre Gert Coetzer, who was left mortified when York referee John Hebblethwaite awarded the Leeds man a penalty try to level the scores. Risman's calm conversion nosed Leeds in front and when he kept his nerve to land the penalty goal in the final moments it seemed as though the Cup was won, but sadly for Fox the game had its one last dramatic twist. Even the Leeds fans and players shared in nationwide sympathy for Fox, whose agony was clear when he was told of his man of the match award live on television by BBC reporter David Coleman. Loiners skipper Mick Clark admitted the circumstances took the gloss off the Headingley club's eighth Challenge Cup triumph. 'Neither side deserved to lose in such conditions,' he told the press after the game. 'We won because we had most of the luck, football skills didn't count for much.' The Challenge Cup was the Loiners' only trophy of the 1967/68 campaign. After finishing top of the league table, seven points clear of Wakefield, they suffered a shock 11-7 home defeat by Wigan – who had finished 14 points back in 11th spot – in the second round of the Championship two weeks before the Wembley final.

Leeds: Risman, Smith, Hynes, Watson, Atkinson, Shoebottom, Seabourne, Clark, Crosby, K. Eyre, Ramsey, A. Eyre, Batten.

Wakefield Trinity: Cooper, Hirst, Brooke, Coetzer, Batty, Poynton, Owen, Jeanes, Shepherd, D. Fox, Haigh, McLeod, Hawley.

LEEDS v. CASTLEFORD

24 May 1969
Odsal, Bradford

Championship final
Referee: Mr B. Thompson (Huddersfield)

Despite doing a league double over Castleford, as Leeds swept to their third consecutive League Leaders' Trophy, it was bruising, uncompromising cup ties between the two arch rivals which left the lingering memory as the decade ended. First blood went to the Loiners at the start of the campaign, with a 22-11 success in the final of the Yorkshire Cup at Wakefield. An over-generous Glassblowers defence had provided John Atkinson and Bernard Watson with easy touchdowns in the first half, Alan Smith and David Hick completing the victory charge as the old trophy resided back at Headingley for the only time in the 1960s. That loss was joyously avenged, however, as Cas eliminated their fierce rivals from the Challenge Cup at the quarter-final stage 'down t'lane' in a match which set the tone for the latter Championship decider. Intensely physical to the point of near open warfare, Leeds snatched a one-point lead in the 50th minute courtesy of Barry Seabourne's long pass and Ray Batten's magical offload which enabled the linking Bev Risman to cross. With Seabourne taking a fearsome battering it looked as though the Loiners had held on until a try barely eight minutes from time by Trevor Briggs dashed their hopes.

Castleford had gone on to raise the trophy at Wembley the week before the Championship showdown, their confidence apparent as they sought to become the first Yorkshire side to do the double since Huddersfield had achieved the feat fifty-four years before. Leeds' league form had been outstanding, losing only three of their regular season fixtures, their most miserly return since 1901/02, but their run to the final had been less than convincing. Oldham put up a spirited fight at Headingley in the first round with hooker Tony Crosby's try just before the interval providing Leeds with the necessary momentum for an ultimately comfortable 32-12 success. Workington's robust forwards gave the Loiners pack plenty to think about in the second round but they were eventually powerless to hold some classic finishing from the home three-quarters with Risman, Atkinson and Mick Shoebottom all on the mark. In the semi-final, Colin Dixon's two excellent long range tries gave Salford justifiable hope of an upset with a six-point lead at the break but the bravery of Seabourne, who defied four dislocated shoulders and numerous trips to the bench for running repairs, and the dexterity of Mick Clark, who carved out tries for Syd Hynes and with fifteen minutes to go for the dynamic Crosby on a thrilling chase, saw Leeds through. Late scores to Ronnie Cowan and Batten eventually inflated the victory margin to 22-12.

The combination of dogged resistence and improvisation needed throughout the three play-off games was to be tested to the limit at Odsal. Talk on the morning of the ultimate clash was about summer rugby, St Helens having proposed a March to November schedule which drew an angry response from Leeds chairman Jack Myerscough. He had written to all the other twenty-nine clubs that day strongly advising them, 'not to be stampeded into the revolutionary and irrevocable step'. The heavy rain which fell in the hour before kick off provided an interesting backdrop to the debate for the 28,442 fans in attendance, many of whom huddled under plastic sheeting and newspapers on the terraces as the deluge swept across the vast bowl. Leeds skipper Seabourne declared himself fit to lead the side out despite his problem shoulder which had barely had time to heal and Ken Eyre returned up front, where it was expected the battle would be won and lost, Mick Joyce dropping into the second-row and youngster Phil Cookson making way.

Leeds 16   Castleford 14

Focused before the toughest of battles, the Leeds side destined to make history as the second one to win the coveted Championship title. From left to right, back row: K. Eyre, M. Shoebottom, B. Watson, B. Ramsey, J. Atkinson, M. Clark. Front row: B. Risman, S. Hynes, R. Cowan, B. Seabourne, A. Crosby, R. Batten, G. Joyce.

Indiscipline in such a highly charged atmosphere was always likely to be a determining factor and Leeds were the first to profit, Cas hooker Clive Dickinson being caught offside and then Keith Hepworth penalised for feeding at the opening scrum allowing Bev Risman to give the blue and amber fans an early chance to vent their support with a successful 35-yard place kick in only the second minute. Loose-forward Malcolm Reilly, fresh from winning the Lance Todd trophy at Wembley, set Castleford on a roll with his first charge, Dennis Hartley carrying it on before Alan Hardisty dropped an equalising goal, his 100th for the club, from a similar distance out to Risman's. Ramsey and Shoebottom made good ground for Leeds, Briggs scampering back to make the tackle and Batten looked like he had created the opening try when he burst through on a fine diagonal run but his pass out wide went to ground.

The pressure on the Castleford line was mounting, Hardisty charging down a drop goal attempt from Seabourne, and Tony Thomas losing possession as the ball spun out of his grasp allowing Syd Hynes to gather and provide for Ronnie Cowan to dive over in the corner to make it 5-2. It was the electrifying Scottish winger's tenth touchdown in eleven games. The lead was short-lived, Dickinson losing and then regaining the ball before pushing his way past four static Leeds defenders close to the line with opposite number Crosby's last ditch despairing tackle helping him over rather than preventing the score. Mick Redfearn's conversion gave Cas a two-point lead after only 13 minutes of intense drama, which had the

---

Leeds: Risman, Cowan, Hynes, Watson, Atkinson, Shoebottom, Seabourne, Clark, Crosby, Eyre, Joyce, Ramsey, Batten. Subs: Langley, Hick.
Castleford: Edwards, Briggs, Howe, Thomas, Lowndes, Hardisty, Hepworth, Hartley, Dickinson, Ward, Redfearn, Lockwood, Reilly. Subs: Bedford, Fox.

THE NORTHERN RUGBY FOOTBALL LEAGUE

League Championship Final

CASTLEFORD v LEEDS

SATURDAY
24th MAY
1969

Kick-off
3.15 p.m.

At
ODSAL STADIUM
BRADFORD

OFFICIAL SOUVENIR PROGRAMME 1/-

trainers from both sides called upon to make numerous visits to the arena – notably to Hynes and Derek Edwards.

With the increased tension came the inevitable simmering physicality, Mick Clark going off to return with a head guard and Keith Hepworth being carried off, although he was later to re-emerge, raising the already white hot temperature. Ramsey and Dickinson were the next to come to blows as both skippers were called out to receive a warning about their side's tactics and future conduct from harassed referee Billy Thompson. A penalty conceded by Joyce gave Redfearn another two points and in reply, after Risman had bravely diffused a kick under his own crossbar, Seabourne's exquisite forty-yard drop goal attempt just bounced back off the post. Interference by Crosby in the tackle saw Redfearn again hit the mark to make it 11-5, but another feeding offence by Hepworth saw Risman claw back the deficit to four points at the interval.

Injuries took their toll in the dressing room casualty station, Cas replacing influential midfield dynamo Reilly who was suffering from concussion after sustaining a series of blows and Leeds losing back line orchestrator Seabourne and stalwart prop Clark as both were forced to give in to their persistent complaints. Another Redfearn penalty hit the post after Ramsey was pulled out for a foul on Brian Lockwood as the vendettas raged, but Hynes relieved the pressure with a timely interception. From the territory gained Risman booted his third goal, the machinations on the pitch spreading to the terraces as five policemen waded into the crowd to quell an outbreak of fighting.

Back on the field, Hardisty worked his characteristic magic, intercepting Joyce's pass on the Leeds 25 to ghost to the line despite Risman's despairing chase which at least pushed him over towards the corner flag. Significantly, Redfearn missed the conversion and Leeds went back on the attack in an effort to salvage the spoils, despite Hynes being a virtual passenger with a leg injury. Cas full-back Edwards pulled off a despairing tackle as Shoebottom, filling in at scrum-half, shot clear from Bernard Watson's superb inside pass, Ramsey keeping the pressure on with a judicious drop goal to make it 14-11. With the Loiners backs seeing more of the ball, they mounted a late, desperate rally but were nearly caught on the counter as Hardisty twice fed the dangerous Thomas only for Cowan to make a despairing try-saving tackle after Redfearn had dragged a difficult penalty attempt wide.

With barely five minutes to go Redfearn's towering kick just eluded chasing Cas substitute Frank Fox and Shoebottom and Eyre scrambled in cover to give Risman a run on his own quarter-way line. A shimmy and dummy past Hartley and away from Briggs took the unbelievably composed full-back to near half-way but up a seemingly blind alley only for his inch perfect kick to the flank to be perfectly read and then magnificently gathered by Atkinson, who raced clear to touch down and level the scores. Risman's next application of the boot for the conversion sealed a dramatic win amid scenes of utter jubilation from the Leeds section of the crowd. There was still time for Hartley to receive his marching orders on the whistle as frustration and venom mounted, the irrepressible and seemingly indestructible Shoebottom the recipient of his ire.

It may not have been a spectacle, more of a dogfight, but that could not detract from the obvious satisfaction in the Headingley camp, Leeds having topped and tailed the decade with the biggest prize after having waited so long for it to arrive in the trophy cabinet. The following Monday, Leeds hosted the traditional W.D. and H.O. Wills Whitsun Sevens, with Castleford being roundly booed on their entrance until it was realised that home wingers Alan Smith and Ronnie Cowan were guesting in their ranks. In a further gesture of solidarity and reparation, for their semi-final against Salford Cas played in Leeds shirts, the Loiners having gone out in the first round courtesy of their weekend celebrations.

LEEDS v. PERPIGNAN

15 November 1969
Headingley

European Club Championship
Referee: Mr R. Thomas (Oldham)

Between 1968 and 1973, Leeds won every honour and trophy open to them at least once. Some maintained an honourable tradition, others were captured for the first time soon after their inception, and one was manufactured. Although perhaps the most prestigious-looking on paper, the European Club Championship was an early exercise in television being the piper that called the tune. The advent of colour demanded a novelty match which could show off the technology to best advantage, and with Headingley a favoured venue it was decided in concert with the BBC that the cross channel champions would face each other. The concept was not a new one, in 1957 Hull and Halifax as Championship winners and runners-up had opposed Carcassonne and Albi home and away. Earlier, in March 1934, Leeds were one of five sides who entertained 'Les Tricolores' on their short tour here before having the compliment returned post season for a quartet of exhibition matches. The following year, Loiners' unbeaten record against French opposition was preserved when Villeneuve were easily defeated at Headingley.

Having survived the Vichy government and proposed and staged the first World Cup in 1954, the French were looking for enhanced domestic competition by the end of the 1960s and were hopeful, prior to this clash, that the top four in each country might compete in a new international league. There was even talk that if this encounter proved to be successful then a contest against the Australian club champions might be next on the agenda. The pre-match hype predicted Leeds' biggest crowd of the season with the club reporting brisk sales of ten shilling stand tickets to welcome a side dubbed as being fast and resourceful with a penchant for running rugby. Little matter that the opposition advertised were a misnomer. Perpignan did have a glorious history – they played in the first Lord Derby Cup final in 1935 and in three of the next five, winning twice – but their name was resurrected for this encounter for ease of reference for the unfamiliar among the watching public. The actual club who came over were double winners XIII Catalan, who drew their players from around the wider Perpignan area.

Not everyone acknowledged the prestigious nature of the challenge with Batley, who were due to play Leeds at home that day, objecting. The Loiners had to agree to travel to Mount Pleasant the following afternoon, causing them to embark on a demanding schedule of five games in ten days. Leeds had Alan Smith returning after injury but Bev Risman was unavailable as he put his academic career first and was on a course at Bath University, with seventeen-year-old John Holmes called in as his replacement.

Perpignan contained three internationals in their line up with veteran Claude Matoulan and tough back-rower Michael Bardes joining their best-known exponent and creative force, Jean Capdouze. A pastry cook by trade, the occupations of his side of part-timers seemed a lot more exotic than their counterparts, Leeds facing a pork butcher, stone mason and cafe owner. Hooker Pierre Rebujent had represented his country at union but Perpignan travelled without three of their top line players and were already struggling to hold onto their domestic crown. A heavy downpour and strong wind affected the crowd but the visitors started well against their sluggish hosts with Capdouze intelligently using the elements. Pendaranda and Holmes swapped penalty misses and with Barry Seabourne starting to exert his midfield influence, Bernard Watson went close down the left.

The visitors' response was swift and dramatic, Capdouze launching Matoulan on a sprint down the right from his own quarter before looming on the inside to take the scoring pass, Pendaranda converting. A strong defensive quarter ended with full-back Praves making a fine

Leeds 31   Perpignan 5

The side were not only Championship winners but also Yorkshire League top dogs in 1969 as Barry Seabourne receives the tin pot at Headingley. Chairman Jack Myerscough looks suitably proud (second from the left) unlike the crouching figure of John Atkinson (extreme right). The reward was to take on the cream of France.

covering effort on John Langley after he intercepted but as the intensity began to wane in the Frenchmen, Leeds responded with a thrilling ten-minute burst that brought them four tries and transformed the contest. Ray Batten and Ted Barnard were the instigators as Seabourne collected a difficult low pass to cross, Holmes converting, before the livewire scrum-half sent Langley in from a perfectly executed scrum base miss move. Before Perpignan could recover, Bill Ramsay kicked over the top of winger Michan and won the race to the ball and John Atkinson rounded off the spree after superb handling among the three-quarters to make it 14-5 at the break.

Injuries meant that both French substitutes started the second half and they had the first thrust through second-row Olet but after that it was all Leeds with Atkinson – who was tormenting opposite number Charcos – unstoppable. Magnificent movement through nine pairs of hands saw Holmes join the line to put Atkinson over, the young full-back's embarrassingly wayward goal-kicking the only blot on the afternoon. Ken Eyre was the next to profit after more mesmerising interplay involving Smith, Ramsay and brother Albert, Atkinson completing his hat-trick between the posts after Seabourne again confused the would-be tacklers. Further spectacular moves brought a fourth try to Atkinson and one to wing partner Smith with Mick Shoebottom the instigator to complete a nine try thrashing. The crowd of 5,145 was judged to be a comparative success but the experiment was not repeated.

Leeds: Holmes, Smith, Langley, Watson, Atkinson, Shoebottom, Seabourne, Barnard, Shepherd, K. Eyre, A. Eyre, Ramsay, Batten. Subs: Hick, Eccles.

Perpignan: Praves, Charcos, Pendaranda, Matoulan, Michan, Capdouze, Clerc, Mas, Rebujent, Peytavi, Olet, Bardes, Humbert. Subs: Courty, Saboureau.

LEEDS v. ST HELENS

15 December 1970
Headingley

BBC Floodlit Trophy final
Referee: Mr E. Lawrinson (Warrington)

The Loiners completed a clean sweep when they beat St Helens to lift the BBC Floodlit Trophy in 1970. Victory in the now defunct tournament, which was played on mid-week evenings and televised live on BBC2, meant Leeds' glorious side of the late 1960s and early 1970s had won every available trophy in the space of four years – League Leaders', the Challenge Cup, Yorkshire Cup, Championship and Floodlit Trophy. Ironically, the Headingley floodlights remained switched off throughout Leeds' BBC final win. The game was played during a power shortage and the Leeds club were refused permission by the electricity board to throw the switch on their £10,000 lights. In the end the game went ahead, illuminated by booster lights powered by the BBC's own generators.

In the five years it was played for before 1970, the Floodlit Trophy wasn't a happy competition for Leeds. Castleford had won it three times and Wigan and Leigh once each, but the Loiners had never even reached the semi-final stage. They began to put that oversight right with hard-fought away victories at Barrow and Widnes, before running in six tries to thrash Hull KR 24-2 in a one-sided semi-final at Headingley. The decider was again staged on home turf and Leeds went into the tie in sparkling form after a run of 10 successive victories, which had seen them run in 276 points.

It was Leeds' second final within a month, following a 23-7 Yorkshire Cup thrashing of Featherstone Rovers at Odsal, when winger Alan Smith had starred with a brace of tries to cap a magnificent run which had seen the Loiners pull off outstanding wins at Wakefield, Castleford and Hull. Saints were league champions after the previous season's 24-12 win over Leeds in the final at Odsal, but were playing their third game in four days and were without both first-choice props Cliff Watson and Albert Halsall, who were out due to injury. Leeds were expecting a bruising battle and they decided not to risk promising young centre Les Dyl, with experienced Scot Ronnie Cowan getting the nod instead. Mick Shoebottom was cleared to play after late checks on a cheek injury suffered in the previous weekend's win at Whitehaven and he continued in the scrum-half role. The Loiners went into the game full of confidence, with football chairman Jack Myerscough declaring: 'We will never have a better chance of winning this trophy. If it doesn't happen this time, we don't deserve ever to win it.'

Myerscough was almost made to eat his words as Saints, who had lost on three of their four previous visits to Headingley, stormed into the lead with a classic try after just 10 minutes. Eric Chisnall, who had been moved from the second-row to prop, showed remarkable pace to leave the Leeds defence flat footed on a 40-yard run, before linking with Billy Benyon, who put the supporting Les Jones over for the opening try. At that stage Saints looked capable of dominating the game, but Leeds rallied in superb style, magnificently led by prop Ted Barnard, who was a tower of strength. Ray Batten and Bill Ramsey were creative in the pack, Bob Haigh, Tony Fisher and John Burke produced huge tackling stints, Tony Wainwright and Shoebottom controlled matters at half-back and Cowan produced a superb show in the three-quarters. Syd Hynes landed a penalty, awarded for an offence by Chisnall, to get Leeds back in the game, but the hosts struggled to find any way through a magnificent Saints defence in the opening half an hour.

The Loiners created a series of half chances, but their finishing let them down until second-row Ramsey struck, running across the visiting defence before slipping out a superb reverse pass to Hynes, who beat John Mantle in a dash to the line. John Holmes converted to give Leeds a 7-3 interval lead. Ramsey, who was inspiring a fine Leeds pack display, and Hynes almost

Leeds 9   St Helens 5

The late Sixties and early Seventies represented a golden age for the club with a host of silverware adorning the Headingley trophy cabinet. Lord Mayor Mr John Rafferty is guest of honour at a presentation night at Harehills Working Men's Club along with Bob Smith ('A' team captain), Ron Cowan, Jack Nelson ('A' team coach), Harry Falkingham (president of the Supporters Club), Mick Clark and Barry Seabourne.

repeated their party piece just after the break, but this time the Saints defence had wised up and the chance was missed. The second half developed into a cat and mouse contest, with neither side being able to prise open the other's defence and the only scoring came from two penalty goals, Holmes extending Leeds' lead and Kel Coslett pulling two points back for Saints. Leeds held on for a 9-5 triumph to the delight of most of the 7,756 crowd, but for once the final had lived up to its billing, the two sides producing a thrilling Rugby League display.

Hynes was quick to pay tribute to the role played by the enthusiastic Headingley crowd, telling reporters: 'Their encouragement was magnificent. It came at the right time and every man in the side felt he could not let down such fine spectators.' Leeds' victory was sweet revenge for the Championship defeat of seven months earlier, but the sides were to get to know each other inside out over the rest of the season. Remarkably, the 1970/71 campaign saw Leeds and Saints' paths clash in every available competition. Honours were shared in the league, with Leeds winning at home and losing by two points at Knowsley Road. Drop goals by Holmes and Shoebottom secured a 4-0 home win in the Challenge Cup second round as Leeds advanced to Wembley, but Saints exacted full revenge in the Championship semi-final with a convincing 22-7 triumph at Knowsley Road. The 1970/71 success proved to be Leeds' only appearance in a Floodlit Trophy final. Their hopes of defending the trophy were ended at the semi-final stage the following season when they were beaten 17-0 at home by…St Helens!

Leeds: Holmes, Smith, Hynes, Cowan, Atkinson, Wainwright, Shoebottom, Burke, Fisher, Barnard, Haigh, Ramsey, Batten.

St Helens: Barrow, Jones, Benyon, Walsh, Wilson, Whittle, Heaton, Rees, Karalius, Chisnall, Mantle, Prescott, Coslett.

Leeds v. Leigh

15 May 1971
Wembley

Challenge Cup final
Referee: Mr B. Thompson (Huddersfield)

According to the pre-match predictions, Leeds only had to turn up at Wembley to win the 1971 Challenge Cup final. The star-studded Loiners arrived beneath the Twin Towers as everyone's tip for the Cup, but departed two hours later as victims of one of the biggest upsets in Rugby League history. More than thirty years on, that May afternoon remains a painful memory for everyone associated with the Headingley club and many of the Leeds fans in the 85,514 crowd are still convinced that Leigh's all-time great Alex Murphy was the villain of the piece.

Murphy was an inspirational figure as player and coach with a host of clubs, including St Helens, Wigan and Warrington, but the Challenge Cup final win over Leeds was his finest hour as he masterminded an incredible giant-killing act. The Leigh scrum-half kicked two drop goals in an inspirational display which earned him the Lance Todd Trophy as man of the match, but he is best remembered for his clash with Syd Hynes which resulted in the Loiners centre becoming the first man sent-off in a Challenge Cup final at Wembley. Player-coach Murphy hit the deck and was stretchered off as referee Billy Thompson pointed Hynes to the changing rooms; however, he returned six minutes later and was fit enough to lift the cup when the final whistle signalled Leigh's 24-7 triumph. Hynes, who was later suspended for six matches, has always protested his innocence and Murphy's role in the incident turned him into a hate figure among fans at Headingley, but the truth is that Leigh would have won the cup even had Leeds finished with 13 men.

The Lancashire outfit led 17-2 when Hynes was dismissed, 15 minutes from time, and they were clearly the better side throughout a miserable afternoon for the Headingley men. The Loiners had been the British game's classiest side throughout the late 1960s and they finished the 1970/71 season in third place in the league, although it's often forgotten that Leigh were just one place and four points behind. Leeds travelled to Wembley looking to win a third piece of silverware, with the Yorkshire Cup and the BBC Floodlit Trophy already on the Headingley honours board. They began their Challenge Cup campaign with a 49-2 hammering of Oldham and they also saw off St Helens, 4-0, and Bramley, 14-0, before a 19-8 victory over Castleford at Odsal in the semi-final, to end the Wheldon Road men's hopes of a third successive final.

At that stage, everything in the Headingley garden was rosy, but just two weeks before the Cup decider tragedy struck when gloriously talented back Mick Shoebottom suffered a career-ending head injury in a Championship second round tie against Salford at Headingley. His loss was a huge blow to the team and the nature of the injury cast a shadow over preparations for Wembley. The gloom at Headingley increased in Leeds' final game before Wembley, when their hopes of a double were shattered by a comprehensive Championship semi-final defeat at St Helens, their first loss in a knock-out tie that season.

A knee injury to play-maker Ray Batten and winger Alan Smith's absence because of a damaged shoulder further disrupted Leeds' preparations, though Barry Seabourne returned from injury after missing all the previous rounds. Generously, Seabourne asked Hynes to continue as captain for the final, but the day itself was a disaster from start to finish for Hynes, his team-mates and the Leeds club. Murphy later claimed he knew the game was in the bag 24 hours before kick-off, when the Leeds team turned up to the traditional Wembley walk-about in jeans and casual clothes, a stark contrast to Leigh, who were smartly turned out in club blazers and ties. Murphy used Leeds' casual appearance as motivation for the Leigh side, telling his team-mates it was a sign the big-time Charlies thought the game was already won. The injury

Leeds 7   **Leigh 24**

Referee Billy Thompson in the thick of the controversial action as Leigh create the biggest upset in Cup final history up to that date. Kevin Ashcroft attempts to wrestle John Atkinson to the floor while Bill Ramsey looks on.

problems forced Leeds into a reshuffle, making four changes from the side which beat Cas in the semi-final. Leigh, whose only previous Challenge Cup triumph had been exactly 50 years earlier, were without the suspended Dave Chisnall and Tom Canning, who was injured, but crucially what they didn't lack was self-belief. Leeds were up against it from the fifth minute when Jim Fiddler gave Leigh the lead with a smartly-taken drop goal.

Welsh winger Stuart Ferguson enjoyed a faultless afternoon with the boot, landing five goals to become only the third man in the sport's history to score in each of his club's games in a season. His first penalty increased their lead before Murphy's pass sent Stan Dorrington over, Ferguson's conversion giving Leigh a shock 9-0 advantage after 25 minutes as the big crowd began to sense an upset could be on the cards. Murphy kept the scoreboard ticking over with a drop goal and another Ferguson penalty on the stroke of half-time sent Leeds in 13 points down. Full-back John Holmes missed a penalty just after the break, but found the target moments later to give Leeds hope. But that was extinguished as Murphy kicked his second drop goal and Ferguson added another penalty to give Leigh a 15-point advantage when Hynes was dismissed. Leeds' misery was compounded when Dave Eckersley landed Leigh's fourth drop goal, a Wembley record, before scooting over for their second try, converted by Ferguson. In the final moments Leeds' teenage stand-off Tony Wainwright made one of their few breaks of the afternoon, but was obstructed by Ferguson as he chased his own kick, referee Thompson awarding a consolation penalty try, which was converted by Holmes. Holmes later admitted: 'It was an awful afternoon for us. All I seemed to do was stand under our posts and watch the goals fly over.'

Leeds: Holmes, Langley, Hynes, Cowan, Atkinson, Wainwright, Seabourne, Burke, Fisher, Bernard, Hick, Haigh, Ramsey. Sub: Dyl.

Leigh: Eckersley, Ferguson, Dorrington, Collins, Walsh, Barrow, Murphy, Watts, Ashcroft, Fiddler, Grimes, Clarkson, Smethurst. Sub: L. Chisnall.

Leeds v. St Helens

20 May 1972
Station Road, Swinton

Championship final
Referee: Mr S. Shepherd (Oldham)

Big-hearted forward Terry Clawson's transformation from villain to hero was the highlight of Leeds' third Championship win in eleven years. Clawson, who played 640 senior games in a professional career which spanned 23 years and nine clubs, blamed himself for Leeds' 16-13 defeat by St Helens in the 1972 Challenge Cup final at Wembley, after he missed three simple shots at goal. Just a week later he defied the boo-boys at Swinton's Station Road to land three kicks, including two from the touchline, as the Loiners were crowned Champions with a 9-5 triumph over the same opponents. And to cap his remarkable personal turnaround, Clawson became only the second Leeds player to win the Harry Sunderland Trophy as Championship final man of the match.

There could be no doubting the right of Leeds and Saints to contest the 1971/72 season's two major cup finals. Leeds, who began the campaign by withdrawing from the Yorkshire Cup in protest at first round ties being played in late July, won 28 and drew 2 of their 34 league games to finish top of the table, beating Saints at Headingley and forcing a 15-15 draw at Knowsley Road. Saints finished five points adrift in third spot, but ended Leeds' hopes of reaching the final of all the knock-out competitions they entered that season with a remarkable 17-0 win at Headingley in the semi-finals of the BBC2 Floodlit Trophy. They went on to win that particular competition and broke Leeds' hearts again as the Loiners lost at Wembley for the second successive year.

The Wembley showpiece saw Leeds make a disastrous start as a defensive blunder handed Saints a first-minute try and the Loiners never fully recovered. The game's decisive moment came in the second half, when Phil Cookson crashed over for Leeds to narrow the gap to three points, only for Clawson to agonisingly miss the conversion from in front of the sticks. The Leeds prop finished the game with a total of five goals to his credit, the same as Saints' Lance Todd Trophy man of the match winner Kel Coslett, but his crucial misses left him in despair. Buoyed by their Wembley triumph, Saints went into the Championship decider just seven days later full of confidence. They were bidding to become only the third side since the Second World War to complete a Challenge Cup and Championship double and they were also on track to be crowned champions for an unprecedented third successive season.

Leeds were forced to make five changes from their Wembley side, with hard as nails forward Tony Fisher moving from hooker to prop for the injured Bill Ramsey and teenager David Ward taking over the No. 9 jersey. John Langley stood in for Syd Hynes in the centres, David Barham replaced scrum-half Keith Hepworth, who pulled out on the day of the game through illness, and Graham Eccles, the day after his 23rd birthday, stepped up off the bench to deputise for Bob Haigh in the second-row. Against exactly the same Saints team which had been on duty at Wembley, the omens for Leeds weren't good, but coach Derek Turner's men responded to adversity with a magnificent, never-say-die team effort to defy all the odds. Clawson's all-round effort and his three nerveless goals saw him hailed as the game's outstanding player, but three of Leeds' stand-ins also made a telling contribution. Young hooker Ward went on to write himself a place in Headingley history as one of the club's greatest and most successful captains. This was the first of his 14 appearances in major finals and he was a revelation, winning the ball in the scrum and performing heroically in the loose. Barham was coolness personified, allying brave defence to steady distribution, and Eccles' toughness and determination shone in the pack. Leeds made the better start, with Ward dominating the opening scrums. Alan Hardisty

Leeds 9   St Helens 5

John Langley and trojan Graham Eccles are mobbed as jubilant Leeds fans invade the Station Road pitch to celebrate Loiners' third Championship triumph.

missed with a drop goal attempt and John Atkinson just failed to reach the same player's grubber kick before Leeds took an 11th minute lead after Saints were penalised for feeding at a scrum and Clawson landed the goal. Alan Smith had to race back to nail Frank Wilson after he intercepted Ray Batten's pass, but Saints kept the pressure on and after John Stephens had been dragged down just short by John Holmes, Leslie Greenall swooped over from acting-half for the first try after 19 minutes.

Ironically, Coslett missed the simple conversion attempt and then, after Holmes was off-target with a drop goal shot, the Saints man fluffed a penalty kick following Eccles' foul on John Walsh. Saints were again penalised for feeding at the scrum, but this time Clawson could not find the target amid a torrent of jeers from the Saints fans. Hardisty missed with another drop goal attempt early in the second half and Saints held their one-point lead until the 54th minute when Clawson finally banished his Wembley demons with a sensational touchline penalty goal, despite the Saints fans' attempts to put him off. Atkinson and Holmes produced desperate try-saving tackles before Leeds struck for the decisive try. Langley was hauled back by Walsh as he chased Ward's kick and from the penalty substitute Fred Pickup's superb off-load picked out Langley and he found Atkinson with a long cut-out pass which sent the Leeds winger tearing over at the corner. That made it 7-3 and Leeds needed the conversion to give them a two-score breathing space. Clawson duly provided it with another wonderful goal from the touchline. Walsh dropped a long-range goal for Saints in a frantic finish, but Leeds held on to claim one of the most satisfying victories in the club's long history. It was the Headingley club's third Championship success and their second in four seasons. Thirty years later they were still waiting for a fourth.

Leeds: Holmes, Smith, Langley, Dyl, Atkinson, Hardisty, Barham, Clawson, Ward, Fisher, Cookson, Eccles, Batten. Subs: Hick, Pickup.

St Helens: Pimblett, Jones, Benyon, Walsh, Wilson, Kelly, Heaton, Rees, Greenall, Stephens, Mantell, Chisnall, Coslett. Subs: Whittle, Earl.

LEEDS v. WIDNES

7 May 1977   Challenge Cup final
Wembley   Referee: Mr J.V. Moss (Manchester)

Triumph tinged with tragedy: two weeks before Leeds pulled off one of the great underdog victories on the biggest stage, the club and its fans had been reeling in shock following the death of young scrum-half Chris Sanderson in the final league fixture at Salford. Signed in 1971 as a promising teenage prospect, Sanderson had just begun to put himself forward as the first choice number seven following Peter Banner's emigration to Australia. Five tries in the previous six championship encounters had thrown down a marker but in a tackle early in the first half at the Willows he was fatally injured. The announcement of his death at half-time caused the match to be abandoned and left many of those present traumatised.

Preparations for the final seemed to pale into insignificance by comparison as Leeds returned to the Twin Towers after a five-year absence to face the then undoubted cup kings, Widnes. Only those who wore the famous blue and amber shirts that day will know how much their resolve and desire was heightened by the loss of one of their own, but it seemed singularly appropriate that the scoring honours went to a precocious nineteen-year-old, amazingly appearing in his first Cup tie, who was deputising for his late colleague. Kevin Dick's supremely confident performance, which saw him completely overshadow vastly experienced campaigner Reg Bowden, would on any other day have won him the Lance Todd trophy, but the vote went to barnstorming Loiners prop Steve Pitchford. His display so demoralised the fearsome Widnes pack that after the game he was selected for Great Britain's squad for the World Cup in the Antipodes, where he inflicted similar damage on the Aussies. Nicknamed the 'bionic barrel' for his upright running stance with chest puffed out to take on all comers, Pitchford ploughed a trail through the middle of the vaunted Chemics six, setting up play in midfield which the sniping Dick and the speedy three-quarters outside him gleefully exploited.

Heavy showers in the lead up to the kick-off meant the impeccable surface was greasy, but the early handling uncertainties only added to the excitement. Within three minutes Dick had already made his mark following up a raking touchfinder to set his bearings with an impeccable 35-yard penalty after he had been fouled by Leeds old boy Bill Ramsey. A rampaging burst up the middle by Pitchford seemed to have released John Atkinson for the opening try, but the prop's lobbed pass was ruled forward. Widnes called on their experience of having appeared in the previous two finals to get themselves into the match with strong runs from back-rowers Doug Laughton and Mick Adams into Leeds territory. Centres Mal Aspey and David Eckersley saw earlier ball as a result and only despairing tackles from Phil Cookson and then Neil Hague kept them out. Pitchford attempted to clear the line with another heroic charge, but Leeds were caught offside and Ray Dutton levelled at 2-2 with a fine 40-yard penalty. In the 19th minute Bowden's clever switch caught out the Leeds defence on the right, Aspey ghosting into space and inside full-back Brian Murrell for a try by the posts which Dutton converted.

That unexpected score seemed to shatter the Loiners' early confidence, Aspey again pressuring the line along with hooker Keith Elwell. A magnificent pass out the back by John Holmes got the Yorkshiremen back on the charge, Stan Fearnley – signed from Bradford just prior to the cup deadline – was the recipient, his clever kick for the line just eluding the supporting Dick. Tigerish captain David Ward's defence kept Leeds in dangerous territory, and on the half hour Holmes' superb early kick for the corner took a wicked bounce to deceive Stuart Wright and stood up perfectly for Atkinson to gather from above the Widnes winger's

Leeds 16   Widnes 7

Ecstasy on the Leeds bench as the final whistle blows. Stan Fearnley ignores the injury that forced him from the fray, Alan Smith looks for a recipient for the contents of the water bucket while coach Syd Hynes and trainer Harvey Standeven leap for joy. Contrasting expressions settle on the Widnes faces.

head to romp to the corner, Dick just missing with the conversion. The Chemics' response was forward led, Jim Mills, Adams and Ramsey all being hurled back from close-in with Pitchford and his unsung fellow prop Mick Harrison battling back up field on the counter attack as the half-time whistle sounded.

Ward's stifling defence and covering made sure that a similar start to the second half, with Mills seeing a lot of the ball, came to nothing. Leeds' best response was a slick move initiated by the mercurial Holmes which ended with a fine tackle by Bowden on Alan Smith. Pitchford was again instrumental in taking Leeds into visiting territory and in the 53rd minute they made the most of it with a classic scrum move. Dick's quick, swept ball from the base gave Holmes

Leeds: Murrell, A. Smith, Hague, Dyl, Atkinson, Holmes, Dick, Harrison, Ward, Pitchford, Eccles, Cookson, Fearnley. Subs: Dickinson, D. Smith.

Widnes: Dutton, Wright, Aspey, Eckersley, O'Neill, Hughes, Bowden, Ramsey, Elwell, Mills, Deardon, Adams, Laughton. Subs: Foran, George.

time and space to work his magic, his deft reverse pass having committed both Widnes centres to him allowing Les Dyl to stride into the hole created and round Dutton on a glorious 20 yard surge to the whitewash. Dick surprisingly missed the conversion but Leeds' one point lead seemed to drain Widnes, their previous territorial dominance having come to nothing. Holmes began to exploit the greater space out wide to telling effect, Murrell sending Smith away only for Dutton and Aspey to bundle him into touch. Dyl stormed clear and Cookson was becoming a menace with his dashing thrusts, Holmes just missing with a drop goal. Another Pitchford rampage just after the hour led to the clinching score.

Cookson, Ward and Fearnley carried on the momentum and Dyl was just pulled down two yards short. From the play-the-ball Dick dummied to pass and gleefully dived past a shellshocked Mills to score between the posts, adding the conversion to make it 13-7. Mills' obvious frustration was taken out on Pitchford but Dick missed the resultant shot at goal. Roy Dickinson's introduction for the injured Fearnley gave Leeds the impetus for victory and with four minutes to go Cookson thought he had scored after another superb lunge only for the Widnes defence to roll him back short of the line. No matter, Dick dropped a goal and with the final kick of a thrilling match landed a penalty. As soon as they had completed their lap of honour, the Leeds players invited Chris Sanderson's widow Sally into the dressing room to join in their celebrations, her grief tempered with the knowledge that the spirited performance was exactly what he would have wanted. Player/coach Syd Hynes revelled in the victory before announcing that he would be hanging up his boots after a glorious thirteen-year career.

A late but exuberant return to Leeds in the early hours of Sunday morning as Phil Cookson and Les Dyl hoist skipper David Ward aloft. Syd Hynes, Graham Eccles, John Atkinson, Kevin Dick and John Holmes join in the frivolity. No doubt a record win bonus of £325 a man helped the party go with a swing.

Hero of the previous afternoon, Lance Todd Trophy winner Steve Pitchford takes due acclaim outside the Civic Hall prior to a mayoral reception.

Leeds v. St Helens

13 May 1978
Wembley

Challenge Cup final
Referee: Mr. B. Thompson (Huddersfield)

The Loiners retained the Challenge Cup in 1978 with a victory over St Helens in one of Wembley's greatest finals. It was only the seventh time in the competition's history that the Cup had been won by the same club in successive seasons and the second time Leeds had achieved the feat after the 1941 and 1942 wartime triumphs. Leeds' road to Wembley began with canine capers at Headingley. An otherwise routine first round win over Halifax became famous after a stray dog invaded the pitch, evading all attempts at capture and hogging the attention of the live BBC cameras. Leeds then turned in an outstanding display to win 28-6 at Wakefield Trinity in the second round before two sensational long-range John Atkinson tries, the first rated among the finest ever scored at Headingley, paved the way for a quarter-final triumph over arch-rivals Bradford Northern after a scoreless first-half. And so to Featherstone Rovers in the last four at Odsal. Leeds were in all kinds of trouble when they trailed 9-7 at the break, but maestro John Holmes scored a wonderful try to conjure up a dramatic second-half fightback. As in 1972, St Helens were Leeds' Wembley opponents and the game followed a similar pattern, but this time with a happy ending for the Headingley men.

Six years earlier Leeds had gone down 16-13 after falling victim to a freak try inside the opening minute. This time Leeds made an even worse start, trailing 10-0 after 13 minutes and 12-5 at half-time, but their second-half rally earned them a place in Wembley history. Leeds were superbly led by braveheart skipper David Ward and powerful second-row Graham Eccles, but their undoubted man of the match was star stand-off John Holmes. One of the finest players of his generation, Homes fittingly was the architect of Leeds' incredible triumph, beginning the move for their first try, having a hand in the second and then providing the final pass for the third. But all that was just an appetiser to his crowning moment, when Holmes landed an astonishing left-footed drop goal to give Leeds the lead for the first time in the closing minutes.

The Leeds man, though, was denied the glory of winning the Lance Todd Trophy for man of the match. Voting took place when it looked like Saints would hang on for victory and their second-row George Nicholls got the nod. It looked as though no Leeds player would even be in contention in the early stages as the error-prone Loiners gifted Saints their big lead. After just five minutes, Harry Pinner's towering kick over the Leeds line bounced out of the grasp of full-back Willie Oulton straight to winger John Atkinson, who also dropped it to present Graham Liptrot with the easiest of tries, Geoff Pimblett adding the conversion. Things went from bad to worse seven minutes later when, after Oulton had missed with a penalty attempt, Bill Francis sliced through the Leeds defence for Saints' second try, Pimblett again adding the extras.

Shell-shocked Leeds finally got their act together when Holmes' long pass sent Mick Crane away and the supporting Les Dyl found Atkinson, who rounded full-back Pimblett in classic style for a superb score, brilliantly converted from the touchline by Oulton. At 10-5 the Loiners were back in the game, but Saints extended their lead before the break when Pimblett kicked a penalty after Eccles obstructed Dave Chisnall in front of the Leeds posts. Oulton missed with his second penalty attempt just before the hooter, but coach Syd Hynes' half-time team talk transformed the game. The holders came out for the second-half firing and skipper Ward got the scoreboard ticking again after just two minutes with a well-taken drop goal. A wretched bounce denied Atkinson as he chased a Holmes kick, but Saints twice went

Leeds 14   St Helens 12

Leeds retain the Challenge Cup after an astonishing, record-breaking, come-from-behind win over Saints. Outstanding skipper David Ward is hoisted on the shoulders of Les Dyl while John Atkinson tries on his new hat for size.

Leeds: Oulton, D. Smith, Hague, Dyl, Atkinson, Holmes, Sanderson, M. Harrison, Ward, Pitchford, Eccles, Cookson, Crane. Subs: Dick, Dickinson.

St Helens: Pimblett, Jones, Noonan, Glynn, Mathias, Francis, Gwilliam, Chisnal, Liptrot, James, Cunningham, Nicholls. Pinner. Subs: Ashton, Karalius.

close as Nicholls and Eddie Cunningham – who later spent a season as a Leeds player – were denied by last-ditch defence. Leeds grabbed their second try when Holmes' pass found Neil Hague and his long ball sent David Smith over at the corner, though he slipped as he attempted to improve the angle and the conversion attempt was missed.

At 12-8 the Loiners were right back in it, but they had a huge slice of luck when a Pimblett drop goal attempt rebounded off a post. One point then could have won it for Saints, but as they began to feel the pace the magnificent Leeds side grew in strength. Into the final 10 minutes Dyl and substitute Kevin Dick went agonisingly close before Phil Cookson knocked on with the line begging. That could have been a killer blow, but the Blonde Bomber made no mistake moments later when he took Holmes' pass close to the opposition line and somehow managed to force his way over, with two Saints defenders tugging on his shoulders and another underneath him trying to hold him up.

Dick volunteered to take the difficult conversion attempt, but Leeds stuck with Oulton, only for the full-back to send his kick just wide to leave the scores level. With five minutes to go Holmes struck his amazing one-pointer to put Leeds ahead for the first time and then Ward repeated the trick in the final moments. But this incredible game had one more twist. With just seconds left Saints regained possession from the re-start and worked an overlap on the right wing near the Leeds line, only for Derek Noonan to knock on with the line at his mercy on the last play of the match. Leeds' stunning fightback saw them become the first side to overturn a 10-0 deficit at Wembley and salvaged an otherwise disappointing season for Loiners, who finished a lowly ninth in the First Division table.

The unsung engine room, Mick Harrison and Roy Dickinson, extol an amazing display of courage, resilience and belief.

Three who played key contributions in the double cup triumph, Kevin Dick, Les Dyl and John Atkinson.

David Ward and Kevin Dick are hoisted on the shoulders of their ecstatic team-mates after the first Wembley triumph in 1977.

LEEDS v. BRADFORD NORTHERN

27 May 1979   Premiership final
Fartown, Huddersfield   Referee: Mr B. Thompson (Huddersfield)

In 1966/67 when Leeds were the League Leaders and claimed the Yorkshire League Championship as the four-tackle rule was introduced, few of even their most fervent fans would have believed that their unbroken run of trophy hoarding seasons would be extended into the decade following. Renowned as a cup fighting side rather than one possessing the necessary consistency – particularly away from Headingley – to mount concerted Championship challenges, they entered the final phase of an inconsistent campaign in 1978/79 relying on the sole knockout option remaining to keep their magnificent run going.

The Premiership had been instituted with the re-introduction of two divisions, a move which had removed the need for a Championship play-off as under the re-structuring all sides in the top division played each other home and away to determine the true champions. Leeds were the inaugural winners in 1974/75 as the format was settled on the top eight, Mel Mason having his finest match in blue and amber as St Helens were comprehensively defeated 26-11 at Wigan with John Atkinson claiming a brace of tries. Four years later, a mediocre start to the campaign had seen the Loiners beaten seven times before Christmas and handed the toughest of draws in the cups. Bradford won by the odd point in 47 in an Esso Yorkshire Cup first round thriller at Odsal, Hull ended hopes in the BBC2 Floodlit Trophy, winning 14-8 at Headingley at the second stage, and there was no respite in the John Player, a trip to Knowsley Road providing the earliest of exits as St Helens triumphed 16-3. A mini-revival in league form in the run up to the Challenge Cup promised justifiable hope of retaining the silverware won the previous two seasons until the balls paired Leeds at their Boulevard nemesis Hull who were jubilant victors 17-6.

If luck had deserted the Loiners in the velvet bag, it returned in the vagaries of the English weather. Late winter heavy snow and deep frost revived memories of 1963, the year that the Headingley management had judiciously decided to install undersoil heating at a cost of £20,000. That investment seemed more than justified sixteen years later as Leeds pressed ahead with their fixtures, playing seven out of eight league matches at home from mid-December to early March. Putting points on the board bred confidence and avoided the lottery of an end of season backlog as the side suffered only two defeats from 13 January to cement fourth spot and, more importantly, have virtually a month's rest before the Premiership began.

St Helens were beaten in the first round at Headingley, Wigan following them five days later which avenged a league double as the Loiners qualified for a showdown with Bradford at Fartown – thereby ending the season as it had begun. Northern had unusually won through to the decider from eighth position, spurred on by a desire to retain the trophy they had won under Peter Fox's guidance against Widnes. Both sides were missing key men; Leeds were without playmaker extraordinaire John Holmes, with Kevin Dick taking his mantle and Sammy Sanderson claiming the number seven shirt after a brace of tries in each of the preceding rounds. Bradford were shorn of finishers David Barends and David Redfearn. Leeds suffered a further setback in the torrid opening exchanges when Les Dyl was forced from the field, coach Syd Hynes producing a masterstroke by unexpectedly switching John Atkinson inside to the centre at key stages in the game.

Bradford's success at that time was built around a big and dominant pack with the likes of Jimmy Thompson, Jeff Grayshon and Len Casey leading the charge. In the early exchanges it

Leeds 24   Bradford Northern 2

Alan Smith, who scored the game-breaking try.

was obvious that their tactics were to outmuscle the Leeds six in the hope of gaining a lead they could defend against the mounting fatigue of their hectic end of season schedule. In contrast, the Leeds half-backs and Dick in particular were determined to run them off their feet, a series of towering, unerringly accurate touchfinders continually turning them around and shunting them back downfield for the scrum. Dick also plagued inexperienced three-quarters Eddie Okulicz and Les Gant with a variety of chip kicks, punts into the space around them and dangerous grubbers to ensure territorial supremacy. An early penalty by Steve Ferres put Northern in front, but that was to be the only time their initially vociferous fans among the near 20,000 throng had anything to cheer about. Leeds were showing the greater invention with the pace of David Smith in the middle worrying the Bradford defence, but they held firm with Keith Mumby and Keith Bridges tackling superbly. The sole try of a typically attritional opening forty minutes was fashioned from an unexpected source, Leeds' Trojan prop Mick Harrison producing a wonderful long pass to allow Neil Hague, linking from full-back, to send David Smith over in the corner in the 32nd minute. It was a move that had nearly worked for David's namesake Alan earlier. Dick's metronomic boot majestically landed the touchline conversion and a penalty soon after put Leeds 7-2 ahead at the break. The tactics were the same in the second period, Bradford's pack aided by the sniping of Alan Redfearn becoming increasingly desperate and weary in their efforts to get past tough tackling Grahams, Joyce and Eccles, in the Leeds back-row while Dick punished their indiscretions with two more penalties and a drop goal to rub salt in their wound.

A final desperate charge saw Dick intercept on halfway and set David Smith free on a wonderful arcing run for glory. Gant earned enormous credit for getting back to haul him down just short but with the Bradford defensive line shot, Alan Smith ghosted in from the wing to acting half-back and tore round to the posts for the game-breaking try. Two further Dick penalties ensured him the Harry Sunderland award, his final tally being 15 points as he converted skipper David Ward's crowning moment, the hooker stepping effortlessly to the whitewash in the closing minutes to complete the rout. A magnificent team performance was rewarded with a then record winning margin to keep the amazing run of success alive and Duraglit on order.

Leeds: Hague, A. Smith, D. Smith, Dyl, Atkinson, Dick, Sanderson, Harrison, Ward, Pitchford, Joyce, Eccles, Cookson. Subs: Fletcher, Adams.
Bradford: Mumby, Parker, Okulicz, Gant, Spencer, Ferres, A. Redfearn, Thompson, Bridges, Forsyth, Trotter, Grayshon, Casey. Subs: Van Bellen, Mordue.

LEEDS v. BLACKPOOL BOROUGH

23 March 1980
Headingley

First Division
Referee: Mr J. McDonald (Wigan)

Now sadly defunct, Blackpool Borough enjoyed just one season in the top flight of British Rugby League. The 1979/80 campaign saw them, not surprisingly, finish rock bottom of Division One, with a record of just 5 wins from 30 matches. The fourth of those wins, though, has gone down in Headingley folklore as possibly the most embarrassing result in Leeds' history. The Loiners were third in the table and still in the hunt for the championship when bottom club Blackpool came to Headingley as sacrificial lambs. No one gave them a chance and most Leeds fans thought the game would be so one-sided it wasn't worth bothering to turn up. Just 4,600, the lowest gate of the season, made the effort, but well before the end they were wishing they too had stayed at home.

It was a disastrous afternoon all round for the Leeds management, who had just announced plans to switch their home fixtures from Saturdays to Sundays the following season. Sunday worst, not best, was just what they didn't need as they attempted to convince the Leeds public that the change was a step in the right direction. Before the game there was nothing to suggest anything unusual was about to happen. Leeds were unbeaten at Headingley all season and were near full-strength, although inspirational duo John Holmes and David Ward were both given a rest, starting the game on the substitutes' bench, with Neil Hague getting a run at stand-off and Gary Hetherington – later to become Leeds chief executive – taking over the hooking role. Ward came on after 33 minutes and Holmes, whose younger brother Phil was in the second-row for the visitors, was eventually introduced at loose-forward nine minutes into the second-half, but by then the writing was already on the wall.

The two-time Challenge Cup winning side of the late 1970s were growing old together and beginning to break up, but Leeds still boasted internationals of the quality of Les Dyl, John Atkinson, Kevin Dick, Roy Dickinson, Steve Pitchford and Dave Heron, plus Eddie Cunningham, in his only season at Headingley, and old-stagers Graham Eccles, Phil Cookson, Willie Oulton and David Smith. The Loiners already had one win over Blackpool to their credit, easing to a 26-8 success in the away fixture five months earlier, but only after Borough had given them a genuine run for their money for the first hour.

Blackpool's season hadn't been all doom and gloom. They had beaten the once-mighty Wigan – destined to go down to Division Two with them at the end of the campaign – at home and won at Workington and high-flying Salford. But the visitors travelled to Headingley in turmoil after sacking their coach just a week earlier and to make matters worse, a nightmare journey over the Pennines saw the team arrive just 15 minutes before kick-off. The entertainers that season, Leeds went into the match as the only side in Division One to have scored more than 500 points – and the 498 Blackpool had conceded made them the top flight's worst defenders. What could possibly go wrong for Leeds? As it happened, everything. What should have been a triumphant procession turned into one of the biggest shocks since the reintroduction of two divisions seven years earlier. Leeds were jeered from the field at half-time, when they led 10-7, and the fans who bothered to stay right until the bitter end weren't slow to make their feelings known. This wasn't a fluke result. Blackpool, inspired by stand-off Alan Fairhurst, were by far the better side and anything other than victory for the visitors would have been a travesty. The Loiners were awful, inept on both attack and defence. The *Yorkshire Evening Post*'s reporter Trevor Watson called it a cabaret, 'an amazing performance of how to make possession disappear'.

Leeds 15   Blackpool Borough 18

LEEDS v. BLACKPOOL BOROUGH

All smiles at the start of the 1979/80 season, the expressions were somewhat different after the disastrous home defeat by unfancied Blackpool. From left to right, back row: H. Standeven (trainer), P. Fletcher, G. Eccles, E. Cunningham, R. Dickinson, S. Pitchford, J. Carroll, G. Hetherington, J. Holmes, A. Smith. Middle row: D. Heron, D. Smith, N. Hague, J. Myerscough (chairman), D. Ward, S. Hynes (coach), L. Dyl, P. Cookson, J. Atkinson. Front row: K. Dick, S. Sanderson.

Time and again Leeds players hurled passes into fresh air. Often, planned moves dissolved into chaos as players ran in entirely the wrong directions. Leeds had every opportunity to post a mountain of points. In the second half they won eight successive scrums, but seven of those possessions was wasted. Six times in the second half Leeds lost the ball on the first tackle. The tries Leeds did manage were impressive efforts, particularly the brace scored by winger David Smith. Centre Cunningham, who had played for St Helens against Leeds at Wembley two years earlier, was one of the few Loiners to emerge with any credit. He grabbed their first try before supporting Heron's excellent break to put Smith over. The home side scored the try of the match in the second period when Hague broke away from a scrum near his own line and Cunningham, Atkinson, Dyl, Atkinson and Cunningham again all linked up in impressive style to support Smith, who went over for his second score, Dick landing his third goal.

But it wasn't even remotely enough. Happy to feed on Leeds' errors, the visitors played neat, tidy, basic football which would have been good enough to avoid an embarrassing defeat in most games and on this occasion was sufficient to pull off one of the sport's great romantic upsets. Fairhurst had an inspired afternoon for Borough, scoring a try and four goals. Full-back John Risman, younger brother of Leeds great Bev Risman who was at full-back for Loiners in the 1968 Watersplash Challenge Cup final, touched down and scrum-half Mick Chester also crossed. The triumph at Headingley is still remembered fondly by Blackpool supporters, but it was their last hurrah at the top level. Borough won just one more match and were relegated at the end of the season. Leeds bounced back from their Blackpool humiliation by winning at St Helens in their next match, to illustrate the agonising inconsistency which makes following the Loiners such a rollercoaster ride. They eventually finished fifth in the table, their only silverware coming thanks to a Yorkshire Cup triumph over Halifax in a final staged at Headingley.

Leeds: Oulton, D. Smith, Cunningham, Dyl, Atkinson, Hague, Dick, Dickinson, Hetherington, Pitchford, Eccles, Cookson, Heron. Subs: Holmes, Ward.
Blackpool Borough: Risman, Saunders, Redford, Mayor, York, Fairhurst, Chester, Gamble, Parry, Molyneux, Lomax, Holmes, Corcoran.

LEEDS v. HULL KR

8 November 1980   Yorkshire Cup final
Fartown, Huddersfield   Referee: Mr R. Campbell (Widnes)

Fewer than 1,000 Leeds fans turned up at Fartown for their side's 1980 Yorkshire Cup final showdown with red-hot favourites Hull Kingston Rovers, but those who stayed away missed one of the Headingley club's greatest triumphs. Leeds were the county cup holders after victory in the previous year's final against second division Halifax, in a match staged at Headingley. But 12 months on it seemed as though their grip on the trophy was about to be prised loose. Those were the glory days of Rugby League on Humberside and Hull KR seemed certain to take yet another big prize back to the county.

The Robins went into the game as Challenge Cup holders and league leaders. Their only defeat of the campaign so far had come in a tour match against New Zealand, although they had dropped a league point in a 1-1 draw with Workington. By contrast, Leeds were languishing near the foot of the First Division and were on a disastrous run of five straight defeats. After hammering York and Hunslet in their opening Yorkshire Cup games, they had come close to embarrassment against Maurice Bamford's Huddersfield in the Headingley semi-final, before scraping through 17-13. Only their remarkable record in cup finals offered Leeds any hope. The previous seven seasons had seen them appear in four Yorkshire Cup, two Challenge Cup and a Premiership final and they had won them all. Leeds also boasted a smart coach in Syd Hynes, whose tactical nous was to prove an inspiration on the day. The Headingley men were without injured centre Les Dyl and big prop Roy Dickinson, but second-row Phil Cookson was passed fit after a head injury and Hynes was able to select from his strongest squad for several weeks, with the fearsome front-row of Mick Harrison, David Ward and Steve Pitchford reunited for the first time in 14 months.

There were no surprises when the team sheets were handed in, but Hynes' masterplan was revealed as the sides lined up for the kick-off. Number one Willie Oulton was on the left wing, with No. 4 Neil Hague switching to full-back and No. 5 John Atkinson in the left centre. Though he didn't know it at the time, Hynes had just invented squad numbers! By moving Atkinson into the centres alongside David Smith, Hynes had come up with a way of countering the speed of Rovers' impressive three-quarter line and the tactic paid off in spectacular fashion. What was expected to be a walkover for Rovers instead became a thrilling end-to-end classic, with Leeds showing incredible spirit to hit back from an early deficit and then defending grimly in the face of wave after wave of Rovers pressure over a nerve-tingling final half hour. Ward set a magnificent lead, superbly backed by Pitchford and Harrison, and half-backs John Holmes and Kevin Dick were outstanding on attack and defence.

Early on it looked as though pre-match predictions would be proved correct as Rovers, backed by the vast majority of the 9,751 Fartown crowd, had Leeds firmly on the back foot, Roy Holdstock and David Hall going close before Atkinson was caught offside, only for Phil Hogan to send his penalty kick against an upright. At the other end David Smith dropped Holmes' pass in a good position and skipper Ward, playing despite a groin injury, was off target with a drop goal attempt. Leeds took a shock lead when Dick landed a penalty after Rovers were caught off-side, but he missed with a similar attempt after Phil Lowe was penalised for a late challenge on Holmes and there was controversy when Holmes' superb pass sent David Smith over, only for referee Ronnie Campbell to award Rovers a penalty for obstruction.

Leeds 8   Hull KR 7

Loose-forward Dave Heron in full flight as underdogs Leeds hang on for a memorable win at Fartown. Graham Eccles, Mick Harrison and Kevin Dick lend their support to the raid.

Rovers made the most of that let-off as centre Mike Smith beat two defenders and shipped out a pass to Gary McHugh who juggled with the ball before touching down for the opening try, converted by Hogan. Things went from bad to worse for Leeds when another obstruction decision gifted Hogan a penalty shot to nudge Rovers into a five-point lead and Dick's attempt to pull two back went wide. Rovers knew another try would put the game beyond Leeds and they should have got it just before the break when Hogan burst clear with a two-man overlap in support, but Oulton produced an astonishing cover tackle to snuff out the danger. Trailing 7-2 at the break, the Loiners found themselves level just two minutes afterwards, thanks to a sensational try by veteran winger Alan Smith and an equally impressive touchline goal from Dick. Smith had become the first winger to win the White Rose trophy as Yorkshire Cup final man of the match 12 months earlier, but his contribution this time was even more valuable as he made the most of good work by Dick and Holmes to hold off two defenders on an irresistible charge to the line.

It was the 300th try of his wonderful career and one of the most important. Dick ignored the jeers of the Rovers fans to land his magnificent conversion and, after Hogan had missed with a penalty shot, the scrum-half sealed the man of the match award with an almost miraculous drop goal from 35 metres out. Still the game wasn't won. Rovers threw everything at Leeds in a desperate attempt to pull the final from the fire, but they were denied at the death by two more remarkable try-saving tackles, Holmes dragging down McHugh before David Heron halted Lowe. The incredible Yorkshire Cup triumph, Leeds' seventh in eleven years, was the only highlight of a poor campaign for Leeds, who slipped back into inconsistent mode in the league, eventually finishing 10th, seven places behind Hull KR.

Leeds: Hague, A. Smith, D. Smith, Atkinson, Oulton, Holmes, Dick, Harrison, Ward, Pitchford, Eccles, Cookson, Heron. Subs: Carroll, Sanderson.

Hull KR: Robinson, McHugh, M. Smith, Hogan, Youngman, Hall, Harkin, Holdstock, Price, Crooks, Lowe, Casey, Crane. Subs: Dunn, Rose.

LEEDS v. WIDNES

3 April 1982   Challenge Cup semi-final
Station Road, Swinton   Referee: Mr F. Lindop (Wakefield)

As is frequently claimed in sport, what goes around comes around. While Leeds fans may well have had sympathy with their Wakefield counterparts at Wembley in 1968, they could not have imagined the true desolation. Fourteen years later, Loiners experienced a similarly sickening feeling as the cruellest of fates denied Robin Dewhurst's men a trip to the Twin Towers. Going into the Challenge Cup semi-final, Leeds had lost only once in the previous nine matches – a comprehensive defeat at Naughton Park – and their cup form had been impressive with York, Barrow and Wakefield all vanquished on their home turf without the men in blue and amber conceding a try. Such doggedness was seen as vital if Widnes were to be overcome at the most callous of hurdles, their reputation as 'cup kings' already well established having been to the final in five of the previous seven seasons and keen to retain the trophy they took from Hull KR.

Leeds opted for size in a bid to hold the Cheshire juggernaut, ostensibly playing with four props and they brought back David Heselwood into the centre, moving youngster Ian Wilkinson onto the wing. Expectation became reality, the opening exchanges robust and borderline and Kevin Dick in no mood to let Andy Gregory run the show in what was to become an intriguing battle of wills. The Leeds pack gained the early ascendancy with rumbling prop Steve Pitchford in the vanguard. Twice he bust the line but the finish was lacking, first when Keith Rayne's low pass eluded Roy Dickinson and then after David Ward supported gamely but could find no scoring outlet. In between Dick claimed the opening points, his penalty punishing Keiron O'Loughlin's high tackle on a menacing Les Dyl.

Although cruelly blighted by injury, there were few finer – or for the opposition, more terrifying – sights than Widnes stand-off Tony Myler in full flight. His grace and balance freed Mick Adams on a diagonal run but the telling pass to Eric Hughes was intercepted by John Holmes and then John Atkinson was called upon to leave his wing to mow Myler down as he stepped clear. In response, Holmes primed his runners to near perfection but the chances went begging, Heselwood and Wilkinson almost reaching the whitewash but the half ended with the margin of the Loiners' advantage tenuous. It was extended after a superb opening to the second half, Keith Rayne and Dickinson both being hauled down just short after more incisive work by the tireless Ward. Dick's blindside dart unsettled the markers and Heron sprang to shimmy past Gregory to make it 5-0. The response was dramatic and effective as the O'Neill brothers and Adams combined to pull the Leeds defence out of alignment, Tony Myler holding off the scoring pass to winger John Basnett until the perfect moment as he created a textbook overlap. Hague's relieving run was more than countered by Stuart Wright's touchline gallop, Adams providing the link for O'Loughlin to again give Basnett room on the outside, the winger needing no second invitation to scorch into the corner, John Myler's conversion – like his earlier penalty attempts – drifting wide.

A point down and barely fifteen minutes left, Leeds brought on the experience of Alan Smith to shore up the defence on the right and Kevin Rayne to replace tiring twin Keith. Holmes tried every magician's trick to prize an opening and with eight minutes remaining he set Kevin Rayne on a charge and although the substitute was held within touching distance of the try line, he somehow squeezed out a pass which Dyl took with glee for a characteristic one-handed touchdown. That Dick's conversion missed seemed immaterial as the clock inexorably ran down. Widnes threw everything at the Leeds line in the frantic closing stages,

---

Leeds 8   **Widnes 11**

Elation one minute, despair the next. Les Dyl powers over for the try which would surely see Leeds at Wembley.

the point of their attacks focusing on Wright who was spectacularly nailed by Heron's cover tackle in the corner and then knocked on with the line seemingly open. Another astute Myler grubber to the in-goal saw the ball bobbing about like a lifebuoy, Holmes hacking it dead to concede the drop out.

The restart was shallow, barely making the thirty metre line but Leeds timekeeper Billy Watts was already preparing himself to officially signal glory. 'Jack Cranston my Widnes opposite shook me by the hand and said, "best of luck at Wembley". I checked my watch and there were 25 seconds left as Adams launched a kick in the direction of the Leeds posts. I remember thinking Neil Hague only needs to take it and if not we only have to survive one tackle.' The punt seemed to spiral upwards in slow motion before, with uncanny accuracy, bouncing off the crossbar into the arms of a startled O'Loughlin. Falling forward and over the line, he won the match in the most dramatic, heartbreaking fashion. Leeds fans were inconsolable as those Widnes supporters who had not left early bemoaning their fate danced with unbridled joy around them. Grown men and women wept openly, others just shook their heads in disbelief while the philosophical smiled and clung on to the phrase – which was repeated like a mantra – that it was just not meant to be.

Leeds: Hague, Wilkinson, Heselwood, Dyl, Atkinson, Holmes, Dick, Dickinson, Ward, Pitchford, Keith Rayne, Burke, Heron. Subs: Smith, Kevin Rayne.

Widnes: J. Myler, Wright, Hughes, O'Loughlin, Basnett, T. Myler, Gregory, M. O'Neill, Elwell, S. O'Neill, Gorley, Prescott, Adams.

LEEDS v. WIDNES

14 January 1984   John Player Trophy final
Central Park, Wigan   Referee: Mr B. Thompson

The headline in the *Rugby Leaguer* the Monday after Loiners' tremendous John Player Trophy final success in a gripping, fiesty contest said it all: 'Leeds set the standards to follow'. John Yates's big match verdict continued, 'Leeds played the kind of fast flowing and inventive rugby which many fans were beginning to think was disappearing from our game. They swept the ball about with pinpoint accuracy and speed ... the standards set by the rejuvenated Leeds should act as a spur to all other clubs.' Perhaps the key word in his eulogy is rejuvenated, as the 1983/84 campaign had opened in disastrous fashion. Crushing defeats at Castleford and home to Hull in consecutive weeks had put any title aspirations in immediate jeopardy but it was the annihilation by a Wally Lewis-inspired Queensland touring team – who played an alien brand of expansive but intimidating rugby to trounce Leeds 58-2 at Headingley – which caused the Headingley faithful to gasp at the realisation of the mountain they had to climb if they were to re-join the code's elite.

The manner of the defeat at Wheldon Road ultimately cost Robin Dewhurst his job as coach when he resigned in its aftermath, the revival stemming from the eventual appointment of immensely proud local boy Maurice Bamford as his replacement. Growing up within a long-range conversion of his beloved Headingley, the opportunity to undertake his dream job yielded immediate dividends but he refused to take any of the credit for the sensational turnaround in fortunes, constantly commenting, 'Coaches don't win matches, the players are the ones who have done it.'

His first game in charge was in the second round of the John Player when one of the favourites for the silverware, Hull KR, were defeated 12-4 in a rousing clash at Headingley. Young full-back Ian Wilkinson claimed a touchdown but the crucial score was a debut try to determined young Kiwi centre Dean Bell in a team display which mixed bravado with a newly found defensive steel. Leeds were indeed fortunate to even be in the competition at that stage, their ignominious win at lowly Blackpool Borough in the opening round coming courtesy of a very late try by John Holmes from a hotly disputed lateral pass in an encounter which left players and fans on both sides intensely exasperated. The quarter-final, a week after defeating the Robins, was another hard-fought success against Second Division opponents with a doughty Swinton side just overcome 16-12 – Wilkinson and Bell again featuring on the scoresheet – in a match notable for the debut off the bench of a player destined to make a massive impact in his short time at the club, Parramatta back-rower Mark Laurie.

A product of the legendary Jack Gibson's school, which saw defence as a primary mode of attack, his textbook tackling seemed to galvanise and inspire the Leeds pack, and none more so than Keith Rayne. The former Wakefield forward, and costliest signing at the time of his arrival, suddenly found his niche at prop and and hit a rich vein of form which eventually played him into Great Britain tour contention. His barnstorming runs, clever offloads and fine support play were epitomised in an outstanding two try display in the second half which saw off Leigh in the Trophy semi-final at Fartown, Huddersfield. Trailing 7-2 at the break, it was Rayne who began the fight back with a rip roaring burst to the line through a clutch of defenders. Although Des Drummond replied with a hotly disputed touchdown in the corner, Rayne then salvaged the tie, helping to create a score for Paul Prendiville before barrelling over from acting-half-back with barely two minutes remaining for the clinching score.

Leeds 18   Widnes 10

£3.00	THE RUGBY FOOTBALL LEAGUE
RESERVED	
SEAT IN SECTION	THE
C	**JOHN PLAYER SPECIAL TROPHY**
	Semi-final
ROW	**Leigh v. Leeds**
R	**SATURDAY, 10th DECEMBER, 1983**
	at Fartown, Huddersfield
SEAT NUMBER	**Kick-off 2-15 p.m.**
№ 16	D, S. OXLEY Secretary General

Success at Fartown with Keith Rayne in outstanding two try form takes Leeds through to the final.

By the time of the Trophy decider a month later, Leeds had remained undefeated, including a heartwarming success against Widnes at Naughton Park in the championship the week before which saw them register 15 unanswered points in a dominant second half display. That, though, was expected to count for nothing with the Chemics maintaining their reputation as the best knock-out side of the era, although they lacked inspirational but sadly injury prone stand-off Tony Myler. All talk in the lead up to the game was of the horrendous weather, the gale force winds the night before reducing one of the posts at Cental Park to half its original size and the hardy band of Leeds fans among the crowd of 9,586 who made the perilous journey across the Pennines caught in showers of drifting snow on the tops. Many were only just rushing through the gates as the black and whites posted the first points, Andy Gregory's expertly timed pass bringing full-back Mick Burke bursting into the line, his inside ball allowing winger Ralph Linton to cross. Burke's superbly judged kick read the elements to perfection, whisking the ball over the bar to make it 6-0.

Laurie's heroic defensive stint led the counter offensive while his balance and step in the cloying midfield continually put the big Widnes pack on the back foot. A penalty from seemingly nerveless teenager David Creasser, in only his 17th match for the club, against the flirtatious wind in the tenth minute signalled a spell of Yorkshire dominance. Outstanding half-backs Holmes – the only survivor from the starting line up when Leeds had last won this cup in 1973 – and Kevin Dick were the architects, sweeping the ball wide to willing runners at every opportunity. Ian Wilkinson, a dominating figure in the Leeds rearguard, sent Paul Prendiville on a touchline scamper and while the Widnes defenders attempted to slow the play-the-ball, Dick put Laurie in motion. His weaving crossfield run found a twinkle-toed Bell in support who committed three desperate cover defenders before producing the perfect inside pass to Holmes to send the mercurial stand-off over, Creasser converting to put Leeds two points ahead.

Leeds: Wilkinson, Prendiville, Creasser, Bell, Smith, Holmes, Dick, Keith Rayne, Ward, Kevin Rayne, Moorby, Laurie, Webb. Subs: Squire, Hague.
Widnes: Burke, Wright, O'Loughlin, Lydon, Linton, Hughes, Gregory, O'Neill, Elwell, Tamati, Gorley, Whitfield, Adams. Subs: Myler, Prescott.

LEEDS v. WIDNES

Coach Maurice Bamford is all smiles in the dressing room after the winning start to his Leeds career is extended. Joining in the celebrations are, from left to right, back row: Ricky Lulham, Andy Smith, Ian Wilkinson, Dean Bell, Kevin Dick, David Ward, Gary Moorby. Front row: Alan Horsfall, Harvey Standeven, David Creasser, Kevin Rayne and Kevin Squire.

With Terry Webb urging his cohorts on and producing some raking kicks, Leeds continued to dictate. Laurie was again the link with a probing run up the left freed by Holmes' latest choice pass, an inside ball to the ever toiling Keith Rayne, and although his quick offload was low and behind the sniping Dick, the scrum-half somehow gathered the ball one handed to roll to the whitewash between the posts. Creasser's conversion made it 14-6 after 22 minutes and Leeds looked set to run riot with David Ward producing a true captain's lead despite injury and Laurie continually mowing down anything that moved in opposing colours. Just after the half hour though, the feelings of disbelief and dejection experienced at Swinton two years earlier seemed to be recurring, with Mick Adams' radar guided boot causing havoc in the blue and amber ranks. His towering bomb was majestically gathered by a spring heeled Joe Lydon who timed his leap to perfection to claim a fine touchdown. Burke's attempt at the extras at the side of the shortened post was deemed wide, television replays appearing to justify the touchjudges' ruling, leaving it 14-10 at the break.

With the freezing conditions worsening, Widnes elected for blunt power to break the Leeds resistance in the second half, Steve O'Neill and Kevin Tamati the ever willing spearheads. Their attempts to gain ground floundered in the arms of the Rayne brothers, Laurie in particular and Webb, while at the back, Wilkinson proved himself imperturbable to a variety of chips, dinks, bombs and punts. The Chemics frustrations visibly heightened, Eric Hughes – deputising for Myler and second best to the wily Holmes all afternoon – was penalised just before the hour for a reckless challenge, Creasser coolly extending the lead to a vital six points.

Discipline was the key in the closing stages, Leeds failing to be intimidated and not conceding a penalty for foul play in the second half while Widnes – with Gregory at his most tortured – incurred Billy Thompson's wrath on nine occasions. Inspirational skipper Ward was reluctantly forced from the fray in the 72nd minute with rib cartilage damage – although nothing was going to stop him from climbing the steps to collect the prize – as Widnes mounted one last concerted attack. Indiscipline again undermined their approach play and five minutes from time Creasser's fifth successful kick sealed the pluckiest of wins. O'Neill was despatched to the sin bin for one indiscretion too many and Laurie, who added this medal to one he had gained four months earlier in similar colours in the Australian Grand Final, capped an overwhelming man of the match performance with a stunning late breakaway.

Ward pointed to the contribution of Bamford as being a key element to the black and gold statue residing in the Loiners dressing room after their poor start to the campaign. 'We had a bit of soul searching to do', he said in obvious discomfort afterwards. 'We all got together, talked it out and things started to go right. Maurice made a difference because he took us back to basics.' The victory was due reward for exceptional teamwork and spirit and deemed especially sweet in the face of attritional provocation. Leeds' unbeaten run was eventually extended to a club record equalling 18 matches but Widnes gained a measure of revenge, again at Station Road, Swinton when they were victorious in the Challenge Cup semi-final in another irascible encounter. Joe Lydon was the hero with two spectacular long range tries although significantly Laurie was a very late withdrawal from the Loiners ranks that afternoon.

Councillor Martin Dodgson, Lord Mayor of the city, congratulates the Leeds squad on their success and unfurls the JPS flag at a civic reception attended by wives and girlfriends. An impromptu collection by Leeds legend Arthur Clues raised £100 for the mayor's appeal for the blind.

Leeds v. Bridgend

27 January 1985
Headingley

Challenge Cup preliminary round
Referee: Mr D. Fox (Wakefield)

In the formative years of the sport, Leeds had occasional encounters with Welsh club opposition. Barry, Pontypridd and Merthyr Tydfil in their transient seasons had all been defeated, with only Ebbw Vale beating the Yorkshiremen – 9-2 in the Principality in December 1907 – their sole success in six meetings between the clubs. Drawn at Headingley in the 1985 Challenge Cup, Bridgend were expected to fare no better, the incarnates of the ailing Cardiff Blue Dragons struggling in the Second Division after the move from Ninian Park to Coychurch Road. Having lost their last three games the season before, they came to Headingley without a win in 17 consecutive matches and with former Rugby Union stalwarts and heroes goal-kicker Steve Fenwick and try machine Tom David having decided to retire.

Two coaches had already been and gone by the time of the thankless draw to face Leeds, Jeff Woods being relieved of the duties after defeat at Sheffield at the end of the previous October and former St Helens and Great Britain prop John Warlow who replaced him lasting barely three months. His frustrations at only getting the players together on match days, and most of those being last-minute loanees, proved too much. Attendances were becoming desperate, with around 2,000 for the opening fixture of the season at home to Swinton having plummeted to 275 for the visit of Carlisle in December. Economically, the cup draw looked like a lifeline but a driving snowstorm in the run up to the kick-off severely curtailed the crowd. Bizarrely, it led to an almost surreal, unforgettable atmosphere at the famous stadium with over 3,500 hardy souls staying on to witness what would be a foregone conclusion. Many had arrived around 1.30 p.m. just as the snow was starting to thicken again but having received assurances that the doughty Welshmen were on their way and that the undersoil heating would ensure play, they staged a mass, impromptu snowball fight on the cricket field. Word of the progress of the Bridgend coach, by now struggling on the M62, was filtered through and by the time they arrived – just after what should have been the scheduled half-time – they were greeted with tumultuous cheers as they turned into the Sharman Gates and around the perimeter. Owing to the delay, the Dragons had changed en route and pronounced themselves ready to play despite having been unable to pick up some of their squad. As a result, they were without proper substitute cover, it being rumoured that the coach driver had been named on the bench.

Leeds' previous foray against Welsh opposition had been 15 years before, when the national side had been beaten at Headingley 28-5 in a trial match and this encounter was never expected to be competitive. It was over as a contest within the first quarter, the Loiners exploiting a back division that contained two unnamed trialists and was without experienced club captain Gordon Pritchard who had begun his career in the blue and amber. By contrast, Leeds had debutant Colin Maskill on the bench, the Great Britain Under-24 international having been signed for a world-record £40,000 fee for a hooker from Wakefield just before the cup deadline. A typical rampaging Trevor Paterson burst opened the scoring wide on the right for the first of his two tries and having found a weakness, the Loiners ruthlessly exploited it. Within 15 minutes, Australian Test winger Eric Grothe, one of the most fearsome sights in Rugby League when in full flight, had grabbed a hat-trick and but for the underfoot conditions and a case of mild hypothermia he may have broken the club record of eight tries in a match. The sight of him diving headlong for the try-line and emerging with his trademark beard having turned white was an enduring image. With the snow continuing to fall heavily, the groundstaff worked tirelessly to continually sweep the lines to enable play to continue with Leeds looking

Leeds 68   Bridgend 6

Bridgend RLFC, 1985.

like scoring on every play. Only the superb punts and hanging re-starts of former grid-iron star and player/coach Dave Alred – subsequently employed by a number of club and international coaches in both codes as a kicking guru – relieved the constant pressure and the defiant tackling of veteran Bob Fleay stemmed the relentless home attacks.

Two of Leeds' emerging teenagers took the opportunity to impress; David Creasser creating a new club points record in the competition with two smartly taken tries and eight goals landed in the most difficult of conditions, while Paul Medley romped away for a brace of touchdowns that were to become his calling cards. Les Dyl returned from a 22-month exile running a bar in Spain to get his name on the scoresheet as did Kevin Dick, back from an injury that had kept him out for five weeks. The only downside for the victors was a serious knee ligament injury to try-scoring stand-off Ricky Lulham. Their best touchdown come late on when full-back Neil Hague waltzed past a bemused, dazzled defence for a picture score.

The biggest cheer of the afternoon, however, was reserved for the battlers from the valleys when former Widnes forward Bob Blackwood struggled over the whitewash for his only points for the club, Alred converting. When referee Fox called a halt to the proceedings slightly early to avoid further punishment, Leeds had amassed their highest score in Challenge Cup football and inflicted the Dragons' largest defeat. The following day Leeds football chairman Harry Jepson, endorsed by skipper David Ward, publicly thanked all those who had attended in such good humour and patience and braved the conditions to create a special atmosphere. A fortnight later, Leeds lost at home to Widnes 14-4 in the tie of the first round proper but for Bridgend it was merely a step towards the end. They won only one game in the remainder of the season, a 28-12 home success over Sheffield, and finished bottom of the Second Division. Having survived one liquidation, they ceased trading at the end of that campaign but not before they had won the hearts of the Headingley faithful for their courage. Seventeen years later, Bridgend Ravens Rugby Union club, led by former Salford and Widnes three-quarter Adrian Hadley, announced their intention to apply for a place in the Super League in 2004.

Leeds: Hague, Grothe, Creasser, Dyl, Hunt, Lulham, Dick, Dickinson, Ward, Hill, Medley, Paterson, Heron. Subs: Holmes, Maskill.

Bridgend: A. Barwood, Alred, A.N. Other, Jenkins, A.N. Other, D. Barwood, Gilmore, Davies, Glover, Thomas, Fleay, Nanson, Vickers. Subs: Blackwood, A.N. Other.

Leeds v. Hull KR

29 March 1986
Elland Road, Leeds

Challenge Cup semi-final
Referee: Mr R. Whitfield (Widnes)

Leeds v. Hull KR
Challenge Cup semi-final replay
Elland Road, Leeds
3 April 1986

Referee: Robin Whitefield (Widnes).

The *Yorkshire Post* called Leeds' 24-24 draw with Hull Kingston Rovers in 1986 a 'semi-final epic of a lifetime' – and it wasn't exaggerating. That breathless encounter in front of an enthralled crowd at Elland Road was a candidate for the Challenge Cup's greatest-ever semi-final – and possibly the finest cup-tie staged outside Wembley. It was a game that had almost everything, a sending-off, a controversial try, two astonishing fight-backs and a nerve-jangling finale. The only thing it lacked was a winner. Leeds led 12-2 against a Rovers side reduced to 12 men following the dismissal of scrum-half Paul Harkin. Incredibly, the Robins rallied to open up a 10-point advantage late in the second half, only for Leeds to come back to snatch a replay.

The sides met again in front of a massive crowd at the same venue less than a week later and, amazingly considering the free-scoring first encounter, played out a scoreless opening half before Rovers powered to Wembley with a dominant display in the final 40 minutes. Ironically, the Loiners' 1986 cup run saw them play four games in Leeds, despite being drawn away in every round. Coached by Peter Fox, the Loiners began their campaign with a 30-8 win at Swinton in the preliminary round – in front of a crowd of just 1,322, the lowest for a Challenge Cup tie involving Leeds – before a 24-4 success over Halifax at Thrum Hall. Tempted by £2,500 and the offer of free coaches for their fans, Doncaster ceded home advantage in round two and gave Leeds a huge fright, leading 10-4 at the break before the relieved Loiners scored 24 unanswered points in the second half.

The third round saw Leeds travel to Widnes and salvage a 10-10 draw with a last-gasp goal by David Creasser, before two penalties and a drop goal secured a 5-0 win in the replay. That set-up a mouthwatering Easter Saturday clash with Hull KR in the last four and for once the game itself lived up to its star billing. The reigning league champions, Rovers had beaten Hull, York and Leigh to reach the semi-final and they drew first blood with a John Dorahy penalty goal after nine minutes. But Creasser replied in kind almost immediately and then the same player grabbed the first try, beating George Fairbairn's despairing tackle after good work by Dave Heron and Neil Hague. Aussie second-row Terry Webb extended the lead with a drop-goal and then, after Creasser had missed a penalty shot, Jeff Grayshon and Kevin Rayne linked to send Tonie Currie away. He was tripped by Paul Harkin as he raced for the corner, but managed to dive over for the try and the Rovers scrum-half was immediately sent-off. Creasser's conversion bounced away off a post, but Leeds led 11-2 and Rovers, who had already lost Chris Burton to a broken arm, were in deep trouble. Chris Lyons added another point with a drop goal, but the Robins narrowed the gap before half-time when David Laws dived over at the corner, referee Robin Whitfield failing to spot he had lost the ball as he attempted to touch down.

It was 12-6 at the break, but Leeds were torn apart in the third quarter to leave their Wembley dreams hanging by a thread. Laws' second try and two Mike Smith touchdowns, all converted by Dorahy, turned the game on its head and Leeds, who had replied with another Creasser penalty, trailed 24-14. But an already sensational cup tie had plenty of twists still to come. First 37-year-old prop Grayshon, seeking his first Wembley appearance, combined with Lyons to

| Leeds 24 | Hull KR 24 |
| Leeds 0 | Hull KR 17 (replay) |

Super sub Paul Medley dives over in classic fashion for the try that tied the scores, only for David Creasser's conversion to slip wide of the posts and send the sides to a replay.

send Currie over for a hope-reviving try, converted by Creasser. Then five minutes later super sub Paul Medley, the 19-year-old hot prospect, latched on to Lyons' pass to storm through Gary Prohm's despairing tackle for the equalising touchdown, though Creasser could not convert.

The final 12 minutes saw more heart-stopping action as both sides went desperately close to the match-winning try and David Ward and Dorahy were both off target with drop goal attempts. A crowd of 23,866 left Elland Road utterly drained, but there was no respite for the players. Leeds, including nine of their cup squad, lost at Bradford the following day and Rovers, who rested all but five of their semi-final heroes, won at Dewsbury twenty-four hours later.

The replay had been set for the Wednesday following the first game, but West Yorkshire police could not provide cover that day and, after the boys in blue rejected a suggestion from the clubs that the game go ahead without police presence, the second match was staged at Elland Road on the Thursday evening. This time an extra 10,000 fans fans turned up and the crowd of 32,485 was the best for a semi-final for 24 years. They were treated to another thriller, for the first half at least. That ended scoreless and it seemed obvious whoever got the first points would go through to Wembley. A minute after the break Harkin went from villain to hero with a crucial drop-goal and from then on the game was always slipping away from Leeds, whose Australian duo Currie and Lyons had cancelled flights home in order to play. Peter Johnson's try and a Dorahy penalty made it 7-0 and after Creasser had missed with a penalty attempt, touchdowns by John Lydiat and Andy Kelly, plus a Dorahy goal, sealed Rovers' 17-0 success. Rovers went on to lose to Castleford in the final and Leeds ended the season empty-handed, finishing sixth in the league, one place above their cup conquerors.

Replay
Leeds: Wilkinson, A. Smith, Creasser, Currie, Gibson, Hague, Lyons, Grayshon, Ward, Powell, Medley, Kevin Rayne, Heron. Subs: Keith Rayne, Webb.
Hull KR: Fairbairn, Clark, M. Smith, Prohm, Laws, Dorahy, Harkin, Johnston, Watkinson, Ema, Kelly, Hogan, Miller. Subs: Lydiat, G. Smith.

Leeds: Wilkinson, A. Smith, Creasser, Currie, Gibson, Hague, Lyons, Grayshon, Ward, Powell, Kevin Rayne, Webb, Heron. Subs: Medley, Keith Rayne.
Hull KR: Fairbairn, Clark, M. Smith, Prohm, Laws, Dorahy, Harkin, Johnston, Watkinson, Ema, Burton, Hogan, Miller. Subs: G. Smith, Kelly.

Wigan v. Leeds

12 December 1987
Burnden Park, Bolton

John Player Trophy semi-final
Referee: Mr R. Tennant (Castleford)

Leeds completed a remarkable metamorphosis when they qualified for the John Player final with a comprehensive win over holders and World Club champions Wigan. Eight months before the near unthinkable had happened for one of the acknowledged giants of the code with only points difference saving the Loiners from relegation out of the top division for the first time at the expense of Oldham. The Headingley board had endeavoured to ensure that the club would never face such ignominy again, re-engaging the services of coach Maurice Bamford the Christmas before after his sabbatical exploits with Great Britain and twice breaking the world transfer record to bring in Lee Crooks and prodigal son Garry Schofield from Hull. Allied to some top Australian talent, of whom stand-off Peter Jackson was the pick, the season had opened in promising fashion although progress in the John Player had been sketchy with narrow victories at Whitehaven, home to Halifax and away at lowly Springfield Borough.

The week before the semi-final, though, Castleford had been trounced 44-0 in a championship encounter in a wonderful display of free-flowing rugby and confidence was high for the clash with the Riversiders. The two sides had already completed their league fixtures against one another with Wigan winning easily at Central Park followed by a thrilling 18-all draw at Headingley. If the Leeds directors needed justification for their outlay it came with the semi-final performance in the unlikely setting of Bolton's atmospheric Burnden Park stadium, in front of a record crowd for that stage of the competition of 13,558. For the Loiners to have any chance against the side who had held the trophy for three of the previous five seasons and were about to embark on an unprecedented run of cup success, they had to have all their big name players on board and firing.

Prospects looked bleak when Crooks – brought back into the side after completing a two-match suspension – badly dislocated his shoulder in the second minute and was forced to leave the fray, Kevin Rayne replacing him. With ferocious defence to the fore, the loss was expected to scupper Leeds' hopes but Australian Test prop Peter Tunks picked up the mantle in probably his best display in Loiners colours to set a true captain's lead. His early diving effort to grass Andy Goodway set the tone after good approach work from ever dangerous Ellery Hanley had set Wigan rolling. Opposite him, Leeds loose-forward Dave Heron replied with a superb long ball to free Schofield and then went on a mazy dart himself from the base of a scrum but defence still dominated. Paul Medley smashed into Hanley as the youngster came of age and the first points were landed when Tunks' indiscretion in the tackle, noted by a touch judge, was penalised. David Stephenson – who was later to join Leeds – potted a fine, angled penalty from 30 metres out.

Soon after, in the 20th minute, Wigan full-back Steve Hampson linked from a scrum, rounded Marty Gurr on the blind side and shot to the corner to make it 6-0. Tunks' animated pep talk behind the posts paid immediate dividends as Leeds swept onto the attack. Heron sent Rayne close and when Ray Ashton switched the play, Medley tore onto the ball through Hampson and Kevin Iro for the touchdown, tireless Colin Maskill's conversion levelling the scores. It stayed that way to the interval with Schofield's attempted drop goal just drifting wide and Roy Powell continuously mowing down the Wigan runners in midfield. Ashton's one-pointer broke the deadlock early in the second half after further forays from Medley and Rayne but the match turned in the 54th minute. Hanley was again the instigator, his run and

Wigan 6	Leeds 19

Colin Maskill and Marty Gurr join in the celebrations as for once Ellery Hanley contemplates the inevitability of defeat.

pass freeing substitute Richard Russell, Stephenson loomed out wide and gave the perfect ball for Henderson Gill to race for the corner. The Great Britain winger, renowned as one of the game's best finishers, appeared to be diving over on the right, but Gurr spectacularly flew headlong out of nowhere to take him into touch with a copybook low tackle.

From that moment belief flooded through the Loiners ranks as they attempted to break their semi-final hoodoo which had seen them defeated in eight successive penultimate matches in the previous three seasons. Just after the hour Schofield produced a moment of world-class magic, ghosting around his man and into a gap out wide before cutting in field to wrong foot Hampson with a delightful swivel of the hips that paid back a huge portion of his transfer fee.

Maskill's conversion made it 13-6, establishing a crucial two-score cushion, and Leeds rammed home the advantage. Gurr's touchfinder maintained the initiative, Ashton had a drop goal attempt touched in flight and the pressure built for a glorious finale. Schofield elected to run on the last tackle teasing the Wigan defence out on the right and producing a great inside pass for winger Steve 'Slippery' Morris to hare for the posts. Confronted by Wigan's best performer Hampson, his lobbed ball found Maskill in support and the happy hooker dived over between the posts and converted for a total of ten points in the game. The scenes of joy and relief that greeted the final hooter were unbounded, Leeds re-establishing their credentials to be considered among the game's elite. Their pack was superb, Medley taking the official man of the match award in a display that virtually booked his place on the tour Down Under the following summer but Powell was not far behind him with a staggering tackle count. He was to produce a similarly colossal effort in the final against St Helens at Central Park and although Leeds dominated large passages of play, they were cruelly sunk 15-14 courtesy of a Neil Holding drop-goal and a brace of tries to rangy centre Paul Loughlin.

Wigan: Hampson, Gill, Stephenson, Lydon, Iro, Edwards, Gregory, Lucas, Dermott, Case, Goodway, Gildart, Hanley. Subs: Russell, Potter.

Leeds: Gurr, Morris, Schofield, Gibson, Basnett, Jackson, Ashton, Tunks, Maskill, Crooks, Powell, Medley, Heron. Subs: Wilson, Rayne.

Leeds v. Castleford

16 October 1988
Elland Road, Leeds

Yorkshire Cup final
Referee: Mr R. Whitfield (Widnes)

Leeds ended their mid-1980s trophy drought with a spectacular win over fierce rivals Castleford in one of the Yorkshire Cup's finest-ever finals. The Loiners went into the game searching for their first taste of silverware since the 1983/84 Regal Trophy triumph over Widnes and a magnificent team performance saw them come up with the goods in a classic showpiece. Castleford, unbeaten so far that season, were the favourites, but a series of long range tries ensured Leeds lifted the trophy for the 17th and final time in front of a 23,000 crowd at Leeds United's Elland Road ground. The victory in Leeds' first County Cup final for eight years and their 21st overall, was a personal triumph for team boss Malcolm Reilly, who had made his name as a player and coach with hometown club Castleford. And it completed a remarkable clean sweep of trophies for Leeds centre David Stephenson. By adding a Yorkshire Cup winner's medal to his collection, the former Wigan man had earned every domestic honour at senior level. Leeds began their cup run in the preliminary round with a 38-16 derby win at Bramley before seeing off Bradford Northern, Wakefield Trinity and Hull, all in tight encounters at Headingley. Cas, who had thrashed Huddersfield 94-12 in the first round before defeating York and Halifax, went into the game in red-hot form and at full-strength after full-back Gary Belcher and prop Kevin Ward passed fitness tests. Leeds kept faith with fireman Gary Spencer at full-back, Aussie Andrew Ettingshausen being handed a wing spot and Lee Crooks getting the nod at prop ahead of giant Kangaroo Test star Sam Backo. Reilly's faith in Crooks was fully justified as the Great Britain man produced one of his finest performances in Leeds colours, combining strong running with punishing defence in a stunning 80-minute effort.

Headingley favourite Roy Powell was outstanding in a non-stop second-row display, while the White Rose trophy for man of the match went to Leeds stand-off Cliff Lyons. The Australian, not yet capped by his country, produced a sensational performance with his creative distribution, clever kicking and effective defence. But the man who will look back on this final with the greatest satisfaction was Leeds centre Garry Schofield. In a magnificent career at international and domestic level Schofield established himself as one of British Rugby League's most complete players of the modern era, but in nine years at Headingley the 1988 Yorkshire Cup provided his only winner's medal.

Fittingly, Schofield put the skids under Castleford with two superb tries in the first half, both coming at times when the Wheldon Road club looked to be getting on top. Cas seemed certain to score when they threw everything at Leeds in a fourth-minute raid, but a remarkable, trademark interception saw Schofield snatch the ball close to his own line and race the length of the field for the opening try. This was converted by Stephenson, who added a penalty before Martin Ketteridge replied with a two-pointer for Cas. Schofield hit back with a drop goal, but Cas looked to be taking control when Giles Boothroyd finished off a sensational handling move for their opening touchdown. Schofield, though, had other ideas, swinging the game back Leeds' way with his second try, from Spencer's pass following a huge break by the rampant Crooks. The evergreen John Joyner, playing in his seventh final, struck back for Cas with a try created by their outstanding winger David Plange and Ketteridge's touchline goal reduced the Loiners' lead to just one point. But that was as good as it got for the Wheldon Road outfit as Leeds began to turn on the power, and by the end the only question mark was over how many points the Loiners would score. Stephenson's second penalty edged them further in front before Carl Gibson got in on the long-range act. It looked as though Leeds must crack as Cas camped

Leeds 32   Castleford 12

The Leeds players do a circuit of Elland Road at the end of the last great Yorkshire Cup final. Two-try hero Carl Gibson (right) and David Stephenson carry the spoils, the latter one of a small, select band to claim a winner's medal in every available rugby league competition.

on their try-line for 18 successive tackles. An incredible one-handed stop by Lyons denied Chris Chapman – who was later helped off after fracturing a bone in a leg – and Ward and Kevin Beardmore were both hauled down when they looked certain scorers. But then Joyner hurled out a long pass, which was intercepted by Gibson and the former Batley winger proved he could match anything done by Schofield by racing 90 metres to the line. Stephenson's conversion meant Leeds led 21-12 and suddenly it was clearly going to be the Loiners' day. That was put beyond all doubt six minutes later when a show of sublime skill by Lyons sent Stephenson away and he supplied Gibson, who evaded full-back Belcher to complete a quick-fire brace, Stephenson rubbing salt into Cas' wounds with the conversion. Twice before in Leeds' Yorkshire Cup run Paul Medley had been a try-scorer after coming off the replacements' bench. The super sub kept up his record with the Loiners' fifth try, striding away to touch down by the flag after taking Lyons' long pass. Stephenson could not convert from wide out, but he did complete the scoring in the final moments with a penalty goal after he was fouled by Keith England. X-rays later revealed Stephenson had completed the game with a badly broken nose as a legacy of that tackle – as well as a Yorkshire Cup final record of six goals to go with his Red Rose final mark of seven, collected during his days at Wigan. Leeds' victory convinced many Headingley fans they were finally assembling a side capable of challenging the likes of Wigan and Widnes for the game's top honours. But though they finished third in the Championship that season, two places clear of Castleford, it was to be another eleven agonisingly long years before Leeds' trophy cabinet was again unlocked.

Leeds: Spencer, Ettingshausen, Schofield, Stephenson, Gibson, Lyons, Ashton, Crooks, Maskill, Waddell, Powell, Brooke-Cowden, Heron. Subs: Backo, Medley.
Castleford: Belcher, Plange, Marchant, Boothroyd, Chapman, Anderson, R. Beardmore, Ward, K. Beardmore, England, Ketteridge, Gibbs, Joyner. Subs: Roockley, Sampson.

CASTLEFORD v. LEEDS

21 April 1991   Premiership first round
Wheldon Road   Referee: Mr J. Smith (Huddersfield)

According to the old saying, the referee is always right. Unfortunately, that isn't necessarily the case and sometimes decisions by the man in the middle can have a crucial bearing on a game. Halifax whistler Jim Smith captured the headlines for an astonishing blunder when Leeds travelled to old rivals Castleford in the first round of the 1991 end of season Premiership. His decision robbed Leeds of a perfectly good try and almost cost them the game, but an amazing last gasp rally saw coach David Ward's men snatch a famous win. Games between Leeds and Castleford are always tense, hard-fought affairs and this one was no exception. Big-spending Leeds had finished fifth in the Stones Bitter Championship, with 14 wins, 2 draws and 10 defeats. Castleford were one place and four points better off, despite honours being shared in league meetings between the two sides. After being hammered 41-16 at Headingley in November, when New Zealander Mike Kuiti scored a hat-trick of tries, Cas had gained revenge with a 16-14 victory at Wheldon Road in February. Coached by Australian Daryl Van de Velde, Castleford's main dangermen were ex-Leeds prop Lee Crooks, ending the regular season in sparkling form, and stand-off Graham Steadman, whose late goal had secured the league win on the same ground two months earlier. Steadman recovered from an ankle injury in time to play in the Premiership tie, but he lasted only five minutes before being stretchered off suffering from a neck injury. Leeds had been a model of inconsistency throughout the campaign, relying heavily on the attacking skills of Great Britain star Garry Schofield and the defensive steel of forward Roy Powell, but travelled to Castleford in confident mood after scoring three tries to two in the league defeat on their previous visit.

Schofield was never far from the headlines and he was at the centre of the thrilling Premiership showdown's most contentious moment, which came in the first half. Leeds were trailing 4-0 to a John Joyner try when Loiners stand-off Schofield intercepted Joyner's pass inside his own half and raced 70 metres for a sensational touchdown. But his joy changed to despair and then anger when he turned around to see referee Smith signalling a scrum for an alleged knock-on. No one else in the ground thought there was a problem and television replays later proved Smith wrong – the ball had been taken cleanly by the Leeds man. Not surprisingly, Schofield returned to the scene of the crime in a foul temper and was sin-binned for his comments to the official. Despite Schofield's spell off the field, Leeds hit back to lead 10-4 at the interval and they would have been further in front had superb breaks by Colin Maskill and Phil Ford been supported during a dominant spell before half-time. Leeds did manage two tries in the first period, Maskill sending second-row Cavill Heugh over before the impressive Paul Dixon stole possession from the hosts and supplied Schofield, whose pass sent Carl Gibson away, the centre beating one tackle before putting Vince Fawcett in at the corner.

The first of Simon Irving's three goals completed Leeds' first-half scoring and the visitors extended their advantage with a long-range Schofield drop goal early in the second period. Cas rallied with a Kevin Beardmore try, converted by Crooks, but then Schofield, whose half-back combination with Paul Harkin was at the heart of most of Leeds' best moments, dropped his second goal and outstanding loose-forward Gary Divorty sent Dixon over, Irving converting to give the visitors an 18-10 advantage. By that stage both sides were down to 12 men, after Maskill and Castleford's Jeff Hardy had been dismissed following a huge brawl.

Castleford 20   Leeds 24

'Schoey' left a host of great memories wearing his cherished colours but few more dramatic than his last gasp try to go with two drop goals at Wheldon Road.

Leeds' eight-point advantage looked to be enough, particularly with the superb Powell marshalling a strong defensive effort. But Leeds fans in the 7,058 crowd were stunned as Castleford rallied in storming fashion to take a 20-18 lead into the final moments. Keith England squeezed over after John Gallagher had failed to take Shaun Irwin's kick, Crooks converting, and then St John Ellis crossed after a great run by Grant Anderson. As the tension mounted, Leeds appeared to have wasted a golden opportunity to snatch a late replay when Gibson was obstructed at a play-the-ball 30 yards from the Cas line.

It looked like a simple kick for Irving, but amazingly Gibson, who up to then had enjoyed a fine match, took a quick tap and Leeds lost possession. That should have been their final chance, but when Leeds lost the ball they were controversially awarded the feed at the resulting scrum, Irving was tackled just short and from acting-half Schofield pushed off one defender and forced his way past two others for a dramatic match-winning try. After the game, Leeds coach Ward revealed Smith – who was due to referee the Challenge Cup final at Wembley the following week – had admitted his first-half error. He told press men: 'As we came out for the second half, I asked the referee what had happened and pointed out he had made a mistake. He said "I'm sorry, I have to hold my hand up, I was wrong." Everybody makes mistakes, if someone is man enough to admit it, then it says a lot for him. Fortunately it didn't make the difference between us winning and losing. We deserved to win.' Hopes of a first Premiership final since 1979 were dashed a fortnight later when Leeds lost 10-7 at Hull. The Loiners led 7-0 at the break and were 7-4 up with two minutes to go, only for Hull to snatch a last-gasp winner after a mistake by the unfortunate Gallagher.

Castleford: Fletcher, Wray, Irwin, Anderson, Ellis, Steadman, French, Crooks, Beardmore, Sampson, England, Hardy, Joyner. Subs: Battye, Larder.
Leeds: Gallagher, Fawcett, Gibson, Irving, Ford, Schofield, Harkin, Powell, Maskill, Wane, Heugh, Dixon, Divorty. Subs: Heron, Lord.

LEEDS v. ST HELENS

26 March 1994
Central Park, Wigan

Challenge Cup semi-final
Referee: Mr J. Holdsworth (Kippax)

For a generation of Leeds fans who had grown accustomed to losing at the most heartbreaking hurdle in the code's premier knock-out competition, victory against St Helens and the odds at Central Park was an almost reverential experience. Not the usual flamboyance, flair and invention ascribed to clashes between these two fierce foes; it was grit, determination, defensive calm, bravery and an almost unshakeable self belief which took Leeds back to Wembley after a drought of sixteen years. The whole cup run had been a glorious ride with the enthusiasm of emerging youth blending perfectly with the settling experience of world class performers gathered together by imperturbable coach Doug Laughton.

Leeds had easily accounted for Rochdale at Spotland in the opening round, five first half tries ending the contest before BBC TV viewers were treated to a sparkling demolition of league leaders Warrington at Headingley. A classic score from former All Black centre Craig Innes after superb handling and a 70 metre dash by Jim Fallon were the highlights of an inspired performance which made the rest of the sides left in the draw sit up and take notice. Both men finished with a brace of touchdowns amid some magnificent close support play where every pass seemed to find its intended recipient.

The same was true in the quarter-final as fiercest derby rivals Bradford were the next drawn to visit Headingley, recalling memories of a classic confrontation at the same stage and venue the last time Leeds had reached the final in 1978. Youngsters Francis Cummins, with a stunning length-of-the-field solo try to raise an incessant visiting siege, and Graham Holroyd, whose interception score on the stroke of half-time visibly sapped Northern's resolve, led the charge. Loiners completely dominated the second half, capping another marvellous all-round performance when hooker James Lowes claimed one of the finest touchdowns seen at the famous venue following length-of-the-field inter-passing between Gary Mercer, Kevin Iro, Innes and Garry Schofield.

Despite the progressive quality of the successive displays which had seen Leeds post 111 points, including 19 tries, and concede only 32, there was concern among Loiners fans when the semi-final pairings were made. The chosen venue of Central Park meant a trip to one of their least favourite grounds, where they had won only twice in the preceding ten seasons, and to face opponents whom they had overcome only once in the previous nine encounters. Such worries appeared to be well founded as Saints dominated possession and field position for almost seventy of the eighty minutes, with youngster Tommy Martyn in his first full season after signing from Oldham and crafty campaigner Kiwi Shane Cooper at the heart of their best moves and Bernard Dwyer a trojan on defence. They could not, however, quell the enthusiasm of Alan Tait who with Mercer passed a late fitness test and set an inspiring lead from the back, the relieving runs of Richie Eyres in his perhaps his best eighty minutes in blue and amber and irrepressible talisman Ellery Hanley. If anyone was going to mastermind a backs-to-the-wall effort and turn it into a glory charge then it was the majestic Loiners skipper, revelling in performing at his magical best on his old stamping ground, despite approaching thirty-three years of age. He will be immortalised for his late brace of touchdowns which finally lifted Saints' siege but his staggering personal tally 42 tackles – out of an equally remarkable team total of 312 – consistently sapped Saints of momentum and confidence and proved to be a crucial factor.

Leeds 20   St Helens 8

The long wait is over. Leeds are on their way to Wembley for the first time in sixteen long seasons. Richie Eyres (left) celebrates the chance to return and put the record straight a year after being sent off in the Challenge Cup final for Widnes, while for Francis Cummins history beckons as the youngest player to appear in the prestigious event.

Although dubbed by many afterwards as an escape to victory, Leeds were never behind, Holroyd opening the scoring in the third minute with a well-struck penalty from wide out. Hasty re-organisation was called for after Fallon's early injury departure, the crowd of over 20,000 in full-throated roar as St Helens powered on to the offensive and monopolised the ball only to find the spirited despairing defence of the Leeds pack impregnable. Lowes was another to finish with 40 tackles from a typically exhaustive effort. On a rare breakout on quarter time, Leeds were gifted a back to back set of six courtesy of Paul Loughlin's mistimed attempted interception of a long Hanley pass. Harvey Howard made good, hard yardage, Schofield weaved to the Saints line and although he was pushed back by David Lyon, the Saints full-back was powerless to prevent Eyres from crashing over through the tightest of gaps sprung by more clever dummy-half play from Lowes. Holroyd's conversion made it 8-0, his two successes contrasting with earlier penalty misses by both Loughlin and Martyn.

The gap, though, was narrowed in the lead up to the break as Martyn dummied to kick on the last tackle and instead swept round Hanley and Tait to the line to bring it back to 8-6. The exuberant Saints stand-off could have been in again before the interval but for a dropped ball with the whitewash beckoning. Worse was to follow for the men from Knowsley Road as they

Leeds: Tait, Fallon, Iro, Innes, Cummins, Holroyd, Schofield, Harmon, Lowes, Howard, Mercer, Eyres, Hanley. Subs: Donohue, Rose.

St Helens: Lyon, Hunte, Ropati, Loughlin, Sullivan, Martyn, Griffiths, Dannatt, Dwyer, Mann, Joynt, Pickavance, Cooper. Subs: Veivers, Harrison.

Coach Doug Laughton and try-scoring skipper Ellery Hanley share the realisation of a dream as the Loiners dressing room erupts in post-match celebrations.

bombarded the Leeds line at the start of the second half forcing more scrambling, last ditch tackles and drop-outs. From a rare Loiners handling error, it seemed that the mounting pressure had finally told with Chris Joynt's long pass sending in Anthony Sullivan at the corner only for referee John Holdsworth to rule that the winger had lost control of the ball before he had grounded it.

Martyn did level matters with a penalty soon afterwards but with Tait weaving more of his relieving magic from the back, Leeds finished in sensational fashion. Eleven minutes from time the Scotsman's mesmerising break saw Hanley loom in inevitable support on the inside to race to the posts before the coup de grace. With Saints summoning every last effort to pen Leeds in their own quarter but unable to turn their seeming supremacy into points, the Yorkshiremen again broke free to spectacularly settle matters. Schofield's long ball on his own twenty metre line was scooped up by Innes who immediately released prodigious youngster Cummins down the flank. He turned the ball inside to a rampaging Iro – living up to his nickname 'Beast' – who drew the remnants of the Saints cover to position Hanley, ghosting up on the inside as usual, to the line. The captain's unbridled joy for his home city was signalled by his iconic double pistol salute while on bended knee behind the posts in front of the ecstatic Leeds fans, their excruciating wait for a trip to London with their side over.

On the final whistle, many of them rushed onto the pitch to chair their doughty heroes from the arena after one of the most courageous and consistent displays of teamwork in the club's history. A jubilant Schofield, whose positional play to scupper Saints' numerous grubber kicks to the line was another key factor in victory, noted amid the euphoria, 'We owed it to the fans. We wanted to do it for the city and the club. It was an incredible feeling seeing Ellery going under the posts at the Leeds end.' Official man of the match Tait was equally effusive. 'Winning the semi was an unbelievable experience' he said. 'The game started well and then seemed to get away from us. St Helens had all the ball and the territory and we just seemed to be constantly tackling. Obviously the pressure on us was great but the longer you hold out, the more the confidence drains from the other side. The relief and emotion in the dressing room told the story.'

A month later, the code's two heavyweight's Leeds and Wigan – appearing in their seventh consecutive Challenge Cup final – surprisingly met for the first time in the competition's decider, with receipts for the game setting a new record when breaking the two million pound mark. The greater experience of the occasion told as the Riversiders raced into a twelve point lead by half-time courtesy of one of the finest touchdowns seen at the Twin Towers as Martin Offiah scorched clear of the cover and turned Tait inside out on an exhilarating 80 metre dash to the try line. Leeds commendably fought back to 12-10 with scores to Fallon and Schofield, but the contest turned on the hour when Wigan brought on two internationals, Mick Cassidy and Sam Panapa, to ultimately wrest control of the game. Consolation for the Loiners was the final touchdown, another spectacular long range solo effort, which went to Cummins, the youngest player to appear and score in a Challenge Cup final. Having waited ninety-nine years to meet on such a stage, Leeds and Wigan then made history the following season when they became the first two clubs to appear at Wembley in successive finals.

Leeds RLFC – Wembley 1994. From left to right, back row: Stuart Walker (physiotherapist), Gary Mercer, Simon Irving, Richie Eyres, Francis Cummins, Paul Cook, Dean Riddle (fitness trainer). Middle row: Doug Laughton (team manager), Graham Holroyd, Marcus Vassilakopoulos, Neil Harmon, Kevin Iro, Harvey Howard, Jim Fallon, Paul Fletcher (alliance coach). Front row: Jason Donohue, Craig Innes, Alan Tait, D.W. Greenwood, CBE (chairman), Ellery Hanley, MBE (captain), R. Shuttleworth (director), Garry Schofield, James Lowes.

LEEDS RHINOS v. ST HELENS

11 April 1997   Super League
Headingley   Referee: Mr R. Connolly (Wigan)

Friday 11 April 1997 was the night Super League finally took off in Leeds. The Headingley outfit were slow to take to the new competition. Summer rugby's inaugural season saw them struggle near the relegation zone, winning just six matches and only escaping the drop thanks to victories in four-pointers over Workington and Paris. The following off-season was marred by a financial crisis and rumours of a move away from Headingley, until new owners Paul Caddick and Gary Hetherington stepped in to save the day. They renamed the club, introducing the Rhinos suffix, switched most home games to Friday evenings and provided cash for new signings – the most significant of those being Iestyn Harris, a £350,000 world record capture from Warrington.

Leeds made a steady start to the 1997 Super League campaign and reached the semi-finals of the Challenge Cup, but defeat by Bradford was followed by a narrow midweek loss at Halifax and then a heart-breaking one-point home reverse to Wigan, when Harris made his first appearance, coming off the substitutes' bench. Saints arrived at Headingley as unbeaten defending champions and Challenge Cup finalists to meet a Leeds team who were desperate for a change of fortune. For the first time, but certainly not the last, Leeds looked to Harris for inspiration, bringing the Welsh international in at stand-off for his first start in blue and amber. Saints had come close to signing Harris before he opted to join Leeds and he seemed determined to show the men from Knowsley Road just what they were missing. Harris went on to play 139 times for Rhinos before a big money switch to Cardiff Rugby Union Club, scoring 1,455 points, but for sheer drama and tension, few of those games matched his first full appearance. With Harris sparkling in the No. 6 role and backed by the majority of a passionate 12,683 crowd, Leeds suddenly found the self-belief which had been so badly lacking over the previous twelve months – and the result was a hugely significant victory, sealed with an echo of the infamous Watersplash Challenge Cup final 29 years earlier. Leeds have played with more flair in Super League, but rarely have they worked so hard or defended so well.

The Leeds pack, superbly led by the outstanding back-rowers Adrian Morley and Anthony Farrell, met Saints' fearsome forwards head-on, refusing to take a backward step and repelling raid after raid with towering defence. The backs worked overtime with centres Richie Blackmore and Phil Hassan and full-back Damian Gibson pulling off a string of try-saving tackles. Chances were few and far between and Saints could point out at the end that they had out-scored their hosts by two tries to one, but for sheer determination and demonstrating a will to win, no one could begrudge Leeds their 13-12 triumph. Almost inevitably, what proved to be the winning point came from the boot of Harris, the stand-off banging over a drop goal seven minutes from time for Leeds' only score of a nerve-tingling second half. But the real drama came in the final moments, when the Rhinos' hard work appeared to have been wasted. There were just seconds remaining when Graham Holroyd kicked out on the full from deep inside Leeds territory as he attempted to clear the home lines and run down the clock. Saints were gifted a lifeline and it looked as though they would take it as former Leeds scrum-half Bobbie Goulding put up a high kick over the Rhinos line – for the only time in the match the home defence hesitated and Goulding took full advantage to regather and touch down, just to the right of the posts.

Goulding's try narrowed Leeds' advantage to just one point with the formality of the conversion, from almost in front of the sticks, still to come. Aware that time was running out,

---

Leeds Rhinos 13   **St Helens 12**

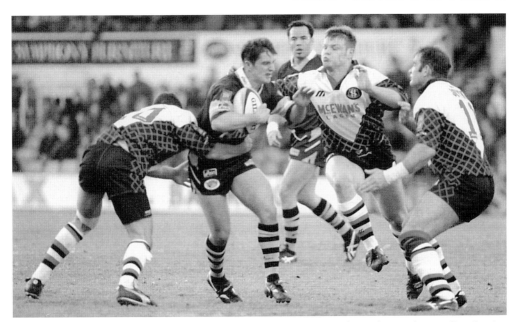

Julian O'Neill and Keiron Cunningham combine to halt the progress of popular Leeds custodian Damian Gibson.

the Saints scrum-half took an age settling himself – and then crashed his kick against the left hand upright to spark uproar among the crowd, not to mention the commentators on the Leeds match-day video, which quickly became a best-seller. The visitors just had time to re-start play, but Leeds snatched possession from a short kick-off and saw out the remaining six tackles with few alarms, the final hooter bringing scenes of incredible celebration on the pitch and the terraces. For jubilant boss Dean Bell it was the best win of his coaching career and his relief at the end was obvious. He told the press afterwards: 'Games like that are few and far between, and we usually lose them. People talk about luck, but luck had nothing to do with it. The players worked hard for the win and they deserved it.'

Defeat, after the disappointments of the previous three games, would have been almost unbearable for Leeds, who had taken the lead for the first time as early as the second minute. Harris and Goulding exchanged penalties before Rhinos' only try of the game, Harris' perfect cross kick picking out veteran winger Paul Sterling. Apollo Perelini crossed for Saints, Goulding equalising the scores with his conversion, but two further Harris penalties sent Leeds in at the break with a four-point lead to set up a nail-biting second period. The victory kick-started a satisfying campaign for Leeds, who pushed eventual champions Bradford Bulls hard and looked destined to finish as well-deserved runners-up before falling away dramatically in the final month to finish fifth. Saints went on to win the Challenge Cup and gained revenge for that Headingley defeat with a 25-18 win at Knowsley Road late in the campaign, but ironically Goulding was again the villain, being sent-off for a high challenge on Rhinos prop Jamie Mathiou.

Leeds Rhinos: Gibson, Sterling, Blackmore, Hassan, St Hilaire, Harris, Sheridan, Masella, Collins, Mathiou, A. Morley, Farrell, Mercer. Subs: Holroyd, Hughes, Newton, Fozzard.

St Helens: Prescott, Arnold, Hunte, Matautia, Sullivan, Martyn, Goulding, Perelini, Cunningham, O'Neill, Joynt, C. Morley, Hammond. Subs: Haig, Northey, Anderson, Pickavance.

Leeds Rhinos v. Adelaide Rams

19 July 1997
Headingley

World Club Championship
Referee: Mr R. Smith (Castleford)

There were many at Headingley who believed that Super League – the move to summer, an expansionist dimension, fashionable marketing, team suffixes and squad numbers – was about as relevant to the game as an ill-conceived idea for British clubs to play their Australian counterparts home and away. Yet when the two came together on a balmy mid-July night, all the old preconceptions were blown away in a carnival atmosphere that saw the Rhinos fully embrace the new era and all it stood for. The trip to the southern hemisphere for the first leg of games a month before had been largely unsuccessful for all the sides from the Old Dart, valuable friendships and contacts being made off the field but little progress on it. Leeds suffered comprehensive defeats at North Queensland (42-20) and on the famous Adelaide Oval (34-8). By the time of the second phase of matches, it was obvious that the decision to involve all clubs from both sides of the world had been overly ambitious, the depth and intensity in the British game distinctly second best to their Antipodean counterparts. Nevertheless, a shirt-sleeved crowd of over 11,000, captivated by the thought of the unfamiliar and exotic, turned up at Headingley in good voice to see the Rams from South Australia. It may not have been the most important fixture staged at the historic venue, but it turned out to be one of the most significant, capped by one of those magical never-to-be-forgotten moments that makes sport so addictive.

New owners Paul Caddick and Gary Hetherington had been slowly rebuilding the fortunes of the famous club, searching for a bolder image and recruiting irrepressible talent Iestyn Harris from Warrington. League results had been good, Leeds were second in the table at the time, but it was the clash with Adelaide – the pre-cursor for the 'Friday night experience' – and the joyous scenes it generated that signalled a justification of the move from Loiners to Rhinos. By the end of the eighty minutes the buzz, heightened by a significant number of face-painted juniors, had reached fever pitch with everyone talking about 'that try' as the hosts took their deserved plaudits. Although captured on film and constantly replayed in the following weeks as the motif for the championship coverage, Paul Sterling's length-of-the-field sprint had to be seen live to be appreciated in its full majesty. It was vital in the context of the game but it was a golden individual career moment for the enigmatic Leeds winger.

Soloman Kiri had put the visitors back in contention at 14-8 on the hour mark when he powerfully tiptoed to the line. The Rams kicked off to the left-hand corner and Sterling began his electrifying charge to immortality from his own in-goal area. Blistering pace and sublime balance saw him burst through the first line of defence, round stranded full-back Michael Maguire and sprint majestically away from the despairing cover dive of Luke Williamson to complete a corner-to-corner dash. Victory was not ensured by such mastery, but a contest that was already simmering was brought to the boil.

It took unerring teamwork to finally wrest the spoils, each of those who ran out behind the Union Jack flag to the strains of 'Land of Hope and Glory' playing their part – particularly in defence. Adrian Morley's performance was colossal despite taking an early knock, Jamie Mathiou relished a rare start with one of his best performances in the colours, and hooker Wayne Collins' midfield organisation was vital to keeping the ship steady. So many of the key confrontations and incidents had him at the centre as he outplayed his illustrious opposite number, former Test star Kerrod Walters. Two other factors which saw the Rhinos home were unpredictable tactics which served to keep Adelaide on the back foot and coach Dean Bell's expeditious use of replacements to keep the impetus going.

Leeds Rhinos 22   Adelaide Rams 14

Chief playmaker Iestyn Harris is just hauled down by the bootlaces as he attempts to spark another attack.

Behind the scrum, defiant try saving tackles from Phil Hassan, Ryan Sheridan and Marvin Golden proved inspirational and Harris revelled in the space created by his elusive running, his return late in the game ensuring victory. His steadying boot which saw him kick five goals was matched by his hand in the other two Leeds tries. Holding a slender 2-0 lead approaching half-time that belied the pressure they had exerted, Rhinos were awarded a scrum on the Adelaide 40 metre line. A quick pass and Harris launched a pin-point kick on the first tackle that sat up obediently for Damian Gibson's perfectly timed chase behind enemy lines. Fourteen minutes into a pulsating second period, after the Rams had clawed back a penalty, Harris was again at the heart of a wonderfully constructed move. Morley powered fearlessly forward, Collins' bludgeoning dart from acting-half-back saw him plunge through three would-be tacklers and almost to the line before Harris' long ball gave Graham Holroyd the chance to deliver a perfect delayed pass allowing Hassan to storm over.

The Aussies were typically stubborn in their resistance, however. Dean Schifilliti's try with ten minutes to go, after Andrew Hick and David Boughton had gone close, made for a tense and exhilarating finish but two Harris penalties, the first following a great break by Terry Newton which saw Bruce Mammando sin-binned, sealed merited victory. Jubilant Rhinos skipper Gary Mercer noted, 'I'd be happy to play in matches like that every week. I haven't seen a better try than Paul's – it was beautiful to watch.'

Leeds: Holroyd, Sterling, Gibson, Hassan, Golden, Harris, Sheridan, Masella, Collins, Mathiou, Morley, Farrell, Mercer. Subs: Rivett, Newton, Hay, Field.
Adelaide Rams: Maguire, Simmonds, Wrigley, Kiri, Grimley, Williamson, Sone, Hick, Walters, Corvo, Galea, Boughton, Blair. Subs: Mammando, Schifilliti, Pierce, Paiyo.

WIGAN WARRIORS v. LEEDS RHINOS

21 May 1998
Central Park

Super League
Referee: Mr S. Cummings (Widnes)

When Wigan's famous Central Park ground was demolished at the end of the 1999 season, Leeds fans were not among those shedding tears for its demise. Central Park was never a happy hunting ground for the men from Headingley. Up to the start of the 1998 season, in 86 visits to play Wigan, Leeds had won there just 15 times, with one draw and 70 defeats: a success record of only 18 per cent. In almost a century of league and cup meetings between rugby league's two most famous clubs, Leeds' biggest victory at Central Park was in the 1973/74 campaign, when they won 29-15.

Wigan dominated British Rugby League for much of the 1990s and though Leeds secured the occasional win over the Cherry and Whites at Headingley, Central Park remained a graveyard. A shock 19-0 win there with an under-strength side in 1991/92 was the exception, but twice in the final decade of the twentieth century Leeds were humiliated on Wigan's home turf. In 1992, Wigan took revenge for that rare blip earlier in the season with a 74-6 rout in a Premiership semi-final, winger Martin Offiah scoring an incredible 10 tries in the Loiners' heaviest ever defeat. Wigan almost matched that embarrassment in the first summer season of 1996, romping to a 68-14 triumph in a year when Leeds flirted with relegation.

So when Leeds travelled to Central Park for a Super League encounter in August 1998, they did so more in hope than expectation, despite impressive league form which saw them vying with Wigan for top spot in the table. Rhinos had been revitalised under their new Australian coach Graham Murray, beginning the league season with a nine-match winning streak which included a memorable 16-8 success over Wigan at Headingley. By August, that remained Warriors' only league defeat. Right from the first whistle of the re-match, it was obvious the 12,786 crowd were in for something special.

Leeds kicked off and as Wigan hooker Robbie McCormack attempted to catch the ball, he was flattened by Rhinos forward Adrian Morley. McCormack played no further part in the game and that incident set the tone for one of the toughest and most intense games seen in Super League. Wigan were furious that Morley wasn't red-carded for his early hit, but the Leeds man didn't stay on the field for long. Mid-way through the first period Morley returned a Wigan drop-out and was hit full in the face by a forearm smash from Warriors back-rower Mick Cassidy, who escaped a sending off but was later banned for six matches after the Rugby Football League's disciplinary committee studied video evidence of the incident. Morley had to be helped from the field with an eye closed and swollen, but he showed incredible courage to return for the game's dramatic finale.

Leeds led 3-0 at half-time thanks to a drop goal and penalty, awarded after Cassidy's foul on Morley, both kicked by outstanding skipper Iestyn Harris. Leeds' magnificent defence didn't yield an inch to Wigan in the first period, but Warriors struck early after the break through an Andy Farrell penalty. If that set Rhinos fans' nerves jangling, they were soon settled when winger Francis Cummins out-jumped Jason Robinson, his Leeds-born opposite number, to touch down Harris' high kick. That was on 51 minutes and the combination struck again just after the hour when Harris slipped out a wonderful pass to send his winger swooping in for the game's second try. Harris couldn't convert either touchdown, but at 11-2 it looked like being Leeds' night at long last.

That belief was severely tested when Wigan struck back, forward Simon Haughton, a regular try scorer against Leeds, racing over for Farrell to convert magnificently from the

Wigan Warriors 8

Leeds Rhinos 15

Barnstorming Adrian Morley's trademark flicked pass means Kris Radlinski's tackle is to no avail.

touchline. With Leeds holding a slender three-point lead the game was back in the melting pot, but Rhinos settled it in spectacular fashion. Australian former international centre Brad Godden was one of Leeds' finest signings of the 1990s and shone brightly through a two-year spell after following Murray to Headingley from Hunter Mariners. That night at Central Park proved to be his finest stand as he clinched an unforgettable victory with a classic try. A Graham Holroyd drop goal attempt was touched by a Wigan player to force a drop-out; the bloodied but unbowed Morley drove the ball back and somehow got out a pass to Godden, who appeared to be hemmed in by a posse of defenders. Incredibly, the half grounded Godden shrugged off a would-be tackler and stepped and shimmied through a mortified defence for the game-breaking touchdown, to spark scenes of incredible celebration among Leeds fans massed behind the posts.

Leeds had conquered their Central Park hoodoo at last. Though they lost there later that season in the Grand Final play-offs, they marked their final visit to the historic old ground a year on with another shock win. Wigan quit Central Park at the end of the 1999 season to move to a new purpose-built stadium, shared with the town's soccer club. The old site is now a supermarket.

Wigan Warriors: Radlinski, Bell, Connolly, Moore, Robinson, Paul, Smith, Cowie, McCormack, Mestrov, Cassidy, Haughton, Andy Farrell. Subs: Clarke, Johnson, Gilmour, O'Connor.

Leeds Rhinos: Harris, Sterling, Blackmore, Godden, Cummins, Powell, Sheridan, Masella, Newton, Fleary, Morley, Anthony Farrell, Glanville. Subs: Holroyd, Mathiou, St Hilaire, Hay.

Wigan Warriors v. Leeds Rhinos

24 October 1998
Old Trafford

Super League Grand Final
Referee: Mr R. Smith (Castleford)

The cavalier manner with which the Rhinos had so comprehensively disposed of St Helens six days previously at Headingley in the final eliminator sent their vast hordes to Old Trafford for the inaugural Super League Grand Final with justifiable optimism of taking the ultimate crown for the first time in 26 years. Having done the double over Wigan in the regular season, a 17-4 reversal at Central Park in the middle of the newly constituted play-off series had seemed to be only a temporary setback and Leeds had got back on track to thoroughly spoil Shaun McRae's last match in charge of Saints. What the blue and amber faithful had not bargained for, though, were the vagaries of the British weather. Throughout the afternoon, incessant rain characteristically streamed out of the gunmetal Manchester sky curtailing all thoughts of expansive play and with it Rhinos' most likely path to victory. Many wondered whether the Grand Final concept would capture the imagination of the Rugby League public used to a first past the post system but with the top two regular season clubs and arguably the biggest in the game meeting centre stage, they need not have worried. An incredible attendance of 43,533 were enticed to Old Trafford at the unfamiliar time of 6.30 p.m. on a Saturday producing a spine-tingling atmosphere as the much trumpeted pre-match entertainment built to a crescendo.

The entry of the gladiators into the imposing arena to a cacophony of noise – the Rhinos fans with their panorama of yellow and blue banners first to erupt at the tunnel end – will never be forgotten by those who were there to witness it. If, after such an emotional initiation, the players had failed to live up to the enormous billing and weight of expectation it would have been understandable, but Herculean effort to the last ensured that the Warriors only claimed the spoils with thirty seconds of the season left on the clock. The outcome may have been different if Iestyn Harris – who finished the campaign as top points scorer in the competition and dominated the opening half – had been successful with two attempts at goal, both of which just shaved the wrong side of the posts on a night that was atrocious for kickers.

Penalties proved to be another determining factor, Wigan winning the count 13-7, although the most telling statistic was that they received eight out of nine between the 10th and 50th minute, denying Leeds vital momentum. Of greater significance, however, was the judicious use of the interchange bench by the Warriors, who made fourteen substitutions in all. There was nothing illegal about the number, with several of the Wigan forwards needing running repairs for cuts during the torrid exchanges, but it meant that John Monie's pack never lost its edge or intensity no matter how hard their Rhinos counterparts strived to wear them down. The defensive effort of both sides was as committed and at times as heroic as anything witnessed in the northern hemisphere – it was attritional rugby of the highest order. Rhinos dominated the opening 35 minutes with clear-cut chances at a premium but twice inspirational skipper Harris found open ground with his mazy runs, the second occasion allowing Ryan Sheridan to put giant Kiwi centre Richie Blackmore outside his opposite number and across for the opening touchdown in the 20th minute.

Similar interplay five minutes later seemed to have unlocked the Wigan defence out wide, but the ball went to ground and with it the Rhinos' chances of what could have been a vital two score advantage in the poor conditions. Even going in 4-0 up at the break would have been a huge psychological boost and due reward for the monumental defensive stints of Marc Glanville, Daryl Powell and Anthony Farrell, but unfortunately 'the one that got away'

Wigan Warriors 10   **Leeds Rhinos 4**

Utter dejection at the final whistle. Coach Graham Murray (far right) contemplates what might have been, flanked by physiotherapist Seamus McCallion and assistant Damian McGrath, while Iestyn Harris, Richie Blackmore and Ryan Sheridan wait uncomfortably for the presentations.

once again came back to haunt them. Wigan fans and officials reckon that the try Leeds-born Jason Robinson scored on the brink of the interval – his devastating pace from the play-the-ball in midfield seeing him shoot to the posts for Andy Farrell to convert – was the most important of his illustrious career in the cherry and white. It certainly broke the hearts of those from his home city. Rhinos hardly deserved to be behind in the dressing room and their mounting sense of frustration was compounded when Farrell added a penalty to give his side breathing space early in the second half.

Forced to play catch up in the torrential rain, Leeds' handling began to look suspect although their defensive commitment never wavered, outstanding scrambling tackles halting Mick Cassidy and Robbie McCormack after Mark Bell had a try disallowed by the video referee for a knock on. Rhinos conjured one final tilt but as he looked set to reach for the line unstinting scrum-half Ryan Sheridan lost control of the ball. In the final minute Graham Holroyd conceded a penalty in his final act in a blue and amber shirt, Andy Farrell landing his third kick to make it 10-4. The Wigan and Great Britain skipper heaped praise on the contest and the concept in the aftermath, 'It was as tough a game as I have ever played in,' he said. 'It was just as intense as a Test match and if that is what Grand Final football is all about, it is definitely going to improve our game.' For the valiant vanquished there was a steely resolve that the big night would be the beginning of a new era. Several quietly mentioned that they would be looking to make amends in the Challenge Cup and history proved them to be true to their word.

.**Leeds Rhinos:** Harris, Rivett, Blackmore, Godden, Cummins, Powell, Sheridan, Masella, Newton, Fleary, Morley, Anthony Farrell, Glanville. Subs: Mathiou, St Hilare, Holroyd, Hay.

Wigan Warriors: Radlinski, Robinson, Moore, Connolly, Bell, Paul, Smith, O'Connor, McCormack, Mestrov, Gilmour, Holgate, Andy Farrell. Subs: Cowie, Cassidy, Johnson, Haughton.

LEEDS RHINOS v. LONDON BRONCOS

1 May 1999   Challenge Cup final
Wembley   Referee: Mr R. Smith (Castleford)

Sometimes a team just know their name is on the Cup. That was the case in 1999 when Leeds Rhinos survived one of the toughest draws in Challenge Cup history to end a decade-long trophy drought and give the old Wembley Stadium a glittering send-off. Leeds smashed a host of records as they crushed London Broncos 52-16 on Rugby League's farewell appearance at the Cup final's spiritual home before the stadium was closed for redevelopment. A memorable day all round belonged to Rhinos' young winger Leroy Rivett, who won the coveted Lance Todd Trophy as man of the match after becoming the first player to score four tries in a Challenge Cup final. Inspirational skipper Iestyn Harris' 20 points and eight goals both equalled Cup final records and Rhinos set new marks for the most points and the biggest winning margin in a decider, though it wasn't all plain sailing as London led 10-0 after 11 minutes and 16-12 early in the second half.

It was a wonderful day for Leeds and their fans, celebrating their first Challenge Cup success for twenty-one years and their first trophy of any kind for a decade, but most of the hard work was done before the final as the Headingley men eliminated all their main rivals on the road to Wembley. Remarkably, all Leeds' matches before the decider were repeats of previous finals. Before the competition began Leeds' players agreed an all-or-nothing bonus deal which would see them receive around £12,000 each for winning the Cup, but nothing if they failed to bring home the trophy.

Rhinos were forced to dig deep right from their opening match, a fourth round tie which saw them drawn at home to Wigan Warriors in a repeat of the previous season's Super League Grand Final. The day after the game, the *Yorkshire Evening Post* described Rhinos' astonishing 28-18 triumph as one of the greatest victories in the club's history – and few people would argue. Beating Wigan in a Challenge Cup tie was momentous enough, but achieving the feat with just twelve players elevated Leeds' triumph to legendary status. Playing their first competitive game of the season, Rhinos were at full-strength and got off to a commanding start as Brad Godden grabbed the opening try, converted by Harris. Skipper Andy Farrell replied with a penalty for Wigan before disaster struck for the hosts at the end of the first quarter as prop Barrie McDermott caught Wigan's Simon Haughton with a tackle around the head and was immediately sent-off by referee Russell Smith. Suddenly it looked like mission impossible for the Rhinos, but their rock-solid defence and all-conquering will to win saw them through.

Leeds adjusted quickly to McDermott's dismissal and Harris extended the home side's advantage with a drop goal before Rivett's wonderful finish powered them further in front. Haughton hit back with a try for Wigan, converted by Farrell, and the game seemed to be swinging the Super League champions' way when Kris Radlinski crossed just before the break to reduce Leeds' advantage to a solitary point. Wes Davies had a touchdown ruled out for a forward pass and Farrell missed with a penalty goal before a Mark Reber knock-on saw a certain try wasted. It seemed to be only a matter of time before Wigan's numerical advantage told, but somehow Rhinos rallied. Cup specialist Ryan Sheridan edged them further in front with a well-taken drop goal and Harris' penalty extended the lead to four points on the hour.

With fans' nerves reaching breaking point, Leeds made the crucial breakthrough 13 minutes from time when Harris and Andy Hay combined to create an opening for Marcus St Hilaire. Harris' conversion gave Leeds a 10-point breathing space and they sealed an

---

Leeds Rhinos 52   London Broncos 16

Murray delight as Rhinos win 'last' Wembley

LEEDS RHINOS coach Graham Murray was "proud and privileged" to be the last man to lift the Silk Cut Challenge Cup at Wembley.

Murray masterminded the Rhinos 52-16 triumph over London Broncos and was fittingly the last man to climb the steps to the Royal Box.

Said Murray: "I was proud and privileged to be part of the day and I was proud and privileged to be lifting the cup for the last time.

Fantastic

"The quality of the football team was always there and I am glad I was able to bring it out.

"The fans were expecting us to win and we delivered. The supporters are magnificent and they were fantastic at Wembley.

The coach added that his side conjured a winning combination of spirit and ability to twice come from behind against the Broncos.

"There is a heck of a lot of skill among these blokes. They are tough and play with a lot of spirit, but there is also a hell of a lot of ability.

"It was a stifling day and I think London held it together for 60 minutes but I was confident we could still come up with a fairly comfortable win."

Murray hoped that the Rhinos had finally shaken off their under-achievers tag.

"There are a lot of blokes that want to play for Leeds. In the past people may have come along for a ride and picked up their cheques," he said.

"But the Darren Flearys, Barrie McDermotts and Anthony Farrells don't come to pick up cheques, they come along to win a game of football and people should be proud of that."

Rhinos hero Leroy Rivett said in bed on Friday and dreamt he would score a hat-trick at Wembley yesterday.

But the flying winger went one better as he grabbed four tries.

"I dreamt that I scored a hat-trick and everything came true," said Rivett. "It truly is unbelievable."

● MATCH REPORT: 2&3

● REACTION: Back Page

● LEEDSING THE WAY: Rhinos players celebrate their record Silk Cut Challenge Cup win over London Broncos.　PICTURE: BRUCE ROLLINSON

Cup delight captured by *Yorkshire Sport*.

unforgettable victory five minutes later when Sheridan dived over from acting-half for another converted try, after Godden had been held just short; Jason Robinson's last-minute score proving scant consolation for Wigan.

A tough fifth round tie at home to St Helens was little reward for Rhinos' magnificent effort against Wigan, but the Headingley men came through a bad-tempered affair to win 24-16 before overcoming Widnes 46-10 away in the quarter-finals. The semi-final saw Leeds paired with arch-rivals Bradford Bulls at Huddersfield's McAlpine Stadium in a repeat of the semi-finals of 1996 and 1997. Leeds had lost both those and it looked like being third time unlucky as Bulls raced into an early 10-0 lead, thanks to tries by David Boyle and James Lowes and a Henry Paul conversion. Had Tevita Vaikona's touchdown not been ruled out for a forward pass, Bulls would surely have won, but from then on it was all Leeds. Harris landed a penalty and then converted a remarkable try by Sheridan, who raced over after stealing the ball from Bulls' Danny Peacock. Another Harris penalty levelled matters at the break and the game hung in the balance until St Hilaire nipped over on the hour, Harris converting. A Sheridan drop goal moved Leeds two scores clear and Harris sealed it with a fine solo touchdown, which he also converted, to spark joyous celebrations on the pitch and among the Rhinos fans.

After such a hard road, Leeds were overwhelming favourites to lift the Challenge Cup against an injury-hit London side making their first appearance in the final and the bookies were proved right, but only after Rhinos were given a real fright. London included Shaun Edwards and Martin Offiah, who had both played a major role in Wigan's long run of Challenge Cup final successes in the late 1980s and early 1990s. Edwards was hampered by a serious hand injury, but it was Offiah who drew first blood, stunning Rhinos with the opening try on just five minutes, Rob Smyth converting.

Leeds Rhinos: Harris, Rivett, Blackmore, Godden, Cummins, Powell Sheridan, McDermott, Newton, Fleary, Morley, Farrell, Glanville. Subs: St Hilaire, Jackson, Hay, Mathiou.

London Broncos: Tollett, Smyth, Fleming, Timu, Offiah, Hammond, Edwards, Retchless, Beazley, Salter, Millard, Simpson, Gill. Subs: Toshack, Callaway, Ryan, Air.

LEEDS RHINOS v. LONDON BRONCOS

Things went from bad to worse for Leeds six minutes later when Karle Hammond, who was Broncos' outstanding player, sent Robbie Simpson over to give London a shock 10-0 lead. A Harris penalty got Rhinos off the mark before Rivett eased Yorkshire nerves with Leeds' first try and Godden, the Aussie centre who gave superb service in a two-year stint, crossed on the stroke of half-time to send them in 12-10 up at the break.

Remarkably, London hit back at the start of the second period through Greg Fleming's converted try, but from then on Wembley belonged to the Rhinos. On 52 minutes McDermott, whose son Billy Lee was the team mascot for the day, completed his transition from Challenge Cup villain to hero when Harris took a quick tap penalty and fed the

A RAMPANT RETURN FOR THE RECORD-BREAKING RHINOS

@ WEMBLEY HEROES: Leroy Rivett and captain Iestyn Harris hold the cup aloft at Headingley as the Rhinos fans go wild

"The fans have been fantastic, both at Wembley on Saturday and welcoming us home to Leeds on Sunday. They certainly helped me along when I made a run for that first try. I just ran for it. "We will try for the double by winning the Super League now we have our confidence." Crowds gathered at Hyde Park in Leeds where the Rhinos players arrived back Turn to Page 3

Comment: Page 6

Drought ends: Back Page

BY ALISON BELLAMY

TRIUMPHANT Leeds Rhinos returned home to a hero's welcome as they held the Challenge Cup high.

More than 17,000 fans were waiting at Headingley Stadium for the Rugby League record-breakers who became the first side to ever score more than 50 points in a Challenge Cup final.

Leeds Rhinos beat London Broncos by 52-16 in the Silk Cut Challenge Cup at Wembley on Saturday.

It is 21 years since the Rhinos last won the cup in 1977 but the wait was worth it. From being 10-0 down the Rhinos steamed ahead to a

jubilant victory in front of their proud fans. More than 50,000 travelled down to see them win.

But the man of the match, 22-year-old winger Leroy Rivett, was the player everyone wanted to see. He too made history by becoming the first man to score four tries at Wembley.

The night before the match he dreamt of scoring a hat-trick but went one better and scored four tries.

He said the thousands of fans who flooded the streets of Leeds had made their homecoming extra special. He said: "I did dream of scoring the night before the match and it came true.

A joyous homecoming reported in the *Yorkshire Evening Post*.

The moment of triumph as Iestyn Harris lifts the famous old trophy to end 21 long years of waiting.

powerhouse forward, who crashed and side-stepped through tackle after tackle on an unstoppable charge to the line. Rivett crossed for his second almost immediately and then the floodgates opened. St Hilaire swooped over for Rhinos' fifth try before Rivett intercepted a pass on his own line to race the length of the field for a glorious hat-trick score, later chosen as the BBC's try of the season. Harris and then Francis Cummins, who had collected runners-up medals in two previous Challenge Cup finals, both touched down, but the last word went to Rivett, whose fourth try earned him a place in Wembley history.

Rivett was suddenly the most famous player in British Rugby League, but sadly his taste of glory was fleeting. Reduced to the role of a fringe player by the end of that season, he was offered another chance in the 2000 Challenge Cup final at Murrayfield, but his mistakes gifted Bradford an early, match-winning lead and he never played for Leeds again. Rivett pipped classy scrum-half Sheridan to the man of the match honour, but Leeds had a team full of heroes as their error-free first-half effort wore London down and allowed their devastating attack to run riot in the final quarter.

Harris was first up the famous Wembley steps to be presented with the Cup by Health Minister Frank Dobson, but the trophy was finally collected by coach Graham Murray, who had transformed Leeds' fortunes in little more than a year at the helm. Leeds dedicated the Cup final win to their massive travelling support, who made up around 50,000 of the 73,242 crowd. Rhinos' sensational triumph gave them high hopes of a Challenge Cup and Super League double, but after fine league wins over Bradford and Wigan they faded badly, eventually finishing third before being eliminated from the play-offs by arch-rivals Castleford Tigers.

Swinton Lions v. Leeds Rhinos

11 February 2001
Gigg Lane, Bury

Challenge Cup fourth round
Referee: Mr C. Morris (Huddersfield)

At the end of this Challenge Cup fourth round tie the Gigg Lane scoreboard read Swinton Lions 10 Leeds Rhinos 6. That would have been arguably the most humiliating result in Leeds' long history, but fortunately for the men from Headingley, this was a game when the scoreboard really did lie. Rhinos had in fact just recorded their highest ever win and only their second three-figure total, but this was just too much for the Bury soccer club scoreboard to cope with, the electronic readout giving up the ghost and clicking back to naught when Leeds hit the century mark. Leeds' final score was actually 106 points, beating by four the total achieved against Coventry way back in 1913, although that 102-0 victory remained by six points the club's greatest winning margin.

The rampant Rhinos, playing their first competitive game of the season, ran in a total of 18 tries, 17 of them converted by Welsh skipper Iestyn Harris for a new club record for number of goals in a game, eclipsing the previous mark of 13 which he shared with Lewis Jones. Eleven of Rhinos' seventeen players got themselves on the scoresheet, man of the match Harris adding a try to his goals tally for a personal total of 38 points. Brett Mullins, Ryan Sheridan, Andy Hay, Anthony Farrell, Kevin Sinfield and Marcus St Hilaire all grabbed a brace of tries, but remarkably no one completed a hat-trick and Tonie Carroll, who was to finish the season at the top of the club's try chart, wasn't among the scorers. Poor Swinton, who had come within moments of a shock Challenge Cup win over Leeds on the same ground five years earlier, simply didn't know what had hit them. Leeds were fresh from a week-long pre-season training camp in Jacksonville, Florida, which had seen them lift the Sunshine State Challenge with exhibition match victories over Halifax and Huddersfield. And they were at full strength, with former Australian Test stars Mullins and Bradley Clyde both in the 17, along with ex-Auckland hooker Robbie Mears and New Zealand World Cup centre Carroll. That in itself proved a notable event. Although Carroll rapidly became a huge favourite with the fans, the other three were all dogged by injury and quit the club at the end of the season. After the huge win at Swinton, the next time all four imports played together was in a Super League defeat at St Helens five months later, and it happened just once more after that. Mears was the first to go, suffering a fractured collarbone just before half-time in the Swinton romp.

Remarkably Swinton had actually levelled the scores after 11 minutes when veteran former Great Britain Test centre Paul Loughlin pounced on a Karl Pratt error. Mick Nanyn, who had earlier got the hosts off the mark with a penalty goal, could not convert and the next time Swinton troubled the over-worked scoreboard was on the hour, when Paul Smith touched down to make it 70-10. Leeds produced an attacking rugby master-class, but all the real excitement came in the final quarter, when players and the 3,239 crowd began to sense that the three-figure barrier could be broken. Leeds were 18 points short with just 12 minutes remaining, but four minutes from time Carroll linked with Marcus St Hilaire to put Clyde over and Harris' conversion brought up the ton. Then in the final moments veteran forward Farrell was the man to make history, accepting Harris' pass to touch down for Leeds' record-breaking score. Farrell had also opened the scoring, again from a Harris pass after just five minutes. After Loughlin's score, Mears scooted over from acting-half to restore Rhinos' advantage and Hay, Mullins and Sinfield all crossed to give Leeds a 28-6 lead after just 28 minutes. The only blot on Harris' remarkable kicking performance came when he failed to convert Sinfield's touchdown, the captain's miss resulting in good-natured jeers from the

---

Swinton Lions 10   Leeds Rhinos 106

Star signing Tonie Carroll, fresh from the World Cup final, ripped the poor Swinton defence apart although he did not make it onto the scoresheet.

Leeds fans. Swinton coach Mike Gregory, a former Great Britain international forward, was labelling his side's effort an embarrassment as early as the 31st minute, when Hay notched his second touchdown. Sheridan and Sinfield both crossed before the interval to give Leeds a 46-6 half-time advantage and normal service was resumed just three minutes after the re-start when Harris dummied over to bring up the half-century.

In cricket, Rhinos would have declared, if it had been a boxing match the referee would have stopped the contest – but this was Rugby League and Rhinos were in no mood to show any mercy. Sinfield, Sheridan and St Hilaire all grabbed their second try and Keith Senior also crossed before Swinton finally managed a response, ironically with the best try of the match as Smith finished off a wonderful move involving a clever chip over the defence, great support and incisive passing. That was brief respite though as tries by Barrie McDermott, Pratt and Mullins took Rhinos into the nervous nineties and Clyde and Farrell rounded off the rout.

The Leeds fans flocked away from Gigg Lane believing they were on course for a glittering season, but it didn't turn out that way. Outstanding wins at Castleford and Hull saw Rhinos through to the Challenge Cup semi-finals, but injuries had kicked in by then and Leeds were pipped 27-22 by St Helens in a thriller at Wigan's JJB Stadium. Aussie Dean Lance, who had been appointed coach at the start of the 2000 season, lasted just one match after that before the axe fell and he was replaced by former player Daryl Powell, who stepped up from his role as head of youth development. The injury jinx, which had first struck when Mears was hurt against Swinton, continued all year and although Leeds finished fifth in Super League, they were eliminated in the first round of the play-offs by St Helens.

Swinton Lions: English, Bateman, Nanyn, Loughlin, Cheetham, Veivers, Peet, Hansen, Barraclough, Barrow, Cushion, Doherty, Smith. Subs: Evans, Napolitano, Hudson, Russell.

Leeds Rhinos: Mullins, Pratt, Carroll, Senior, Cummins, Harris, Sheridan, Fleary, Mears, McDermott, Hay, Farrell, Sinfield. Subs: St Hilaire, Walker, Clyde, Mathiou.

Bradford Bulls v. Leeds Rhinos

9 February 2002
Valley Parade

Challenge Cup fourth round
Referee: Mr R. Smith (Castleford)

Rarely, if ever, can a Leeds side have been rated as such underdogs as in this cup tie. Odds of 20-1 with leading bookmakers, who were also offering an 18-point start to the men from Headingley, signified the degree of difficulty at hand. In some respects the pessimism was justified, Bradford were unbeaten at their Valley Parade home – and undefeated in the city for eighteen months – and only the week before had embellished their Super League crown by adding the World Club Challenge and the justifiable claim to be the best side in the game. Their demolition of crack Australian outfit Newcastle Knights, like that of Wigan in the Grand Final, had been another awesome eighty minute performance based around a formidable, relentless pack so that even the expectancy of the most ardent Rhinos fan must have been tempered by realism. Nevertheless, those who travelled and populated the Symphony end were in good voice, and were particularly looking forward to seeing the full debuts of new Australian recruits Ben Walker and Matt Adamson. Both were to have massive impacts from the kick-off, the former Penrith second-rower clearly relishing the physical encounter and dominating his opposite numbers with his powerful bursts and punishing defence. Walker's invention and distribution were quickly on show with Leeds, whose short kicking game had once been a weakness, were now spoilt for options.

That was evident in the seventh minute when Ryan Sheridan – again reserving one of his very best performances for the Challenge Cup – grubbered to the in-goal for Walker to perfectly time his run for the touchdown, his conversion making it 6-0. The much vaunted Bradford pack ran into a brick wall in the Leeds front-row, with Barrie McDermott consistently driving them back with his relieving runs. Matt Diskin, taking over the mantle from the side's most consistent player in 2001 Robbie Mears, proved that the faith of the coaching staff was justified as he more than matched Bradford's key orchestrator James Lowes and Darren Fleary looked back to his best of the Graham Murray era, intimidating the home forwards with his shuddering tackling. Behind them, Kevin Sinfield showed how much he had benefitted from inclusion in the previous autumn's Ashes series against the Kangaroos with a controlled and mature display bossing the midfield alongside Sheridan.

A second Walker penalty at quarter time took the lead to eight points and raised the real spectre among the visiting supporters, whose tireless band played louder as the contest progressed, that maybe the outcome was not going to be the foregone conclusion predicted by many. Just as that realisation began to dawn the Bulls hit back, Daniel Gartner brushing aside Adrian Vowles on a scamper to the corner with Marcus St Hilaire receiving treatment and out of the line. It was a rare mistake for the former Castleford skipper in a highly encouraging debut out of his favoured position, deputising for Tonie Carroll in the centre. His front-on defence was commanding, forcing the Bradford three-quarters across the field to try and escape his clutches and making a crucial tackle late on when he forced bustling winger Lesley Vainikolo into touch at the corner when seemingly on his way to a certain try. Bradford's prop rotation of their 'awesome foursome' had ground down the majority of opponents in their period of domestic dominance but Stuart Fielden and Paul Anderson were overshadowed by Rhinos' debutant pair Wayne McDonald and in the crucial, nerve-jangling latter stages Willie Poching.

The opening score of the second period was always going to be of immense psychological importance especially as the Leeds six showed no signs of wilting in the face of the expected

Bradford Bulls 4   Leeds Rhinos 17

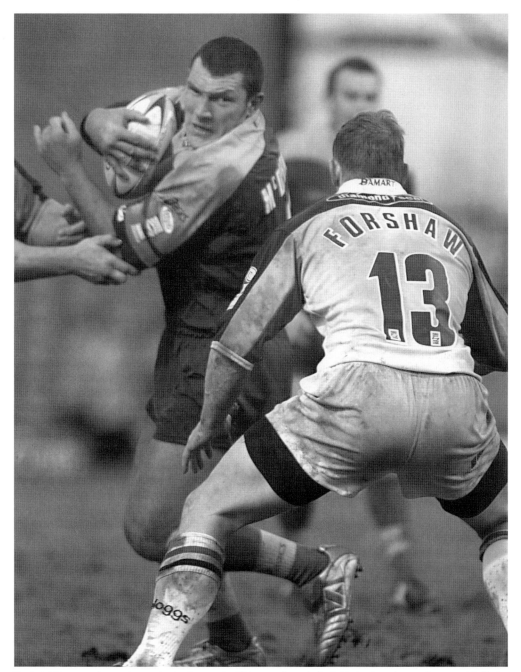

Barrie McDermott charges into Mike Forshaw as the Rhinos pack steals the initiative from the much vaunted Bulls six.

Bradford Bulls: Withers, Vaikona, Naylor, Gilmour, Vainikolo, Paul, Deacon, Vagana, Lowes, Brian McDermott, Peacock, Gartner, Forshaw. Subs: Fielden, Anderson, Pryce, Costin.

Leeds Rhinos: Cummins, St Hilaire, Vowles, Senior, C. Walker, B. Walker, Sheridan, Fleary, Diskin, Barrie McDermott, Hay, Adamson, Sinfield. Subs: Poching, McDonald, Burrow, Jones-Buchanan.

Bradford Bulls v. Leeds Rhinos

Matt Adamson celebrates a stunning debut with Chev Walker, the Australian's fearless runs into the heart of the action setting the platform for a memorable victory.

Bradford barrage. Leon Pryce, on for injured talisman Robbie Paul, showed the frustration of the hosts when he was put on report and subsequently banned for an out of character attack on Sinfield and a minute later Sheridan calmly dropped a goal to push Leeds five points clear. For the Rhinos fans desperately clinging to thoughts of an unlikely upset in front of the watching millions on the BBC, the second half seemed to last for hours but as the minutes ticked by, their heroes got stronger. Rob Burrow, on at hooker in place of Diskin, scurried busily among the bemused Bulls, Adamson – playing the full 80 minutes for the first time in ten years – grew in stature and McDermott's re-introduction signalled the final push, but what heartened the blue and amber army most was the teamwork. A needless obstruction by the hapless Pryce following a harmless kick through gave Walker the chance to give Leeds breathing space and with the aplomb of his immediate predecessor Iestyn Harris he duly obliged with the telling two points, giving his side a precious two score cushion.

The contest ended in perfect symmetry for the Rhinos, with a try seven minutes from the end and in-front of their by now elated fans. It was scored, inevitably, by the undoubted man of the match, Sheridan timing his run from deep to perfection to skittle three would-be challengers from 15 metres out in a drive to the whitewash that would not be denied, Walker again converting to claim 12 points in all. There was still time for one last dramatic act as the Bulls threw everything into attack. It seemed that Brandon Costin had escaped on the right flank to power over in the corner and set the pulses racing only for the diminutive Burrow to somehow fly across in an act of defiance that summed up the resolve of his team-mates to force him into the corner flag. For new recruit Adamson there was no disguising the joy and emotion. 'It was everything I expected it would be. We knew it was going to be tough right to the end but it is a great way to start the season for the club and the fans. Today was a crucial game to set a standard for the season and I thought we did that.' Unfortunately for Rhinos, that optimism vanished in the semi-final when St Helens put on a mesmerising masterclass to convincingly take them to Murrayfield.